JOB

JOB

The Story of a Holocaust Survivor

by

Joseph Freeman

PARAGON HOUSE
St. Paul, Minnesota

Published in the United States by

Paragon House
2700 University Avenue West
St. Paul, Minnesota 55114

Library of Congress Cataloging-in-Publication Data

Freeman, Joseph, 1915-
    Job : the story of a Holocaust survivor / by Joseph Freeman.
      p. cm.
    Includes bibliographical references (p.)
    ISBN 1-55778-823-5 (pbk. : alk. paper)
    1. Freeman, Joseph, 1915- 2. Jews—Poland—Radom (Radom)—Biography.
    3. Holocaust, Jewish (1939-1945)—Poland—Radom (Radom)—Personal narratives.
      4. Holocaust survivors—Biography. 5. Radom (Radom, Poland)—Biography. I.
      Title.
    DS135.P63 F64 2002b
    940.53'18'092—dc21

                                                                      2002012058

                        10 9 8 7 6 5 4 3 2

                    www.paragonhouse.com

Dedication

This book is dedicated to my children who suffered so much growing up under the shadow of the Holocaust.

I would also like to express my deepest appreciation to Rebecca and Seymour Fromer from Magnum Museum in Berkeley, California, who inspired me; to Shalmi Barmori, educational director from the Israeli Holocaust Museum Yad Uashem, who opened my eyes to look at the Holocaust from a different perspective—as a member of a free society; to Professor Michael Nutkiewicz, director of the Martyrs Memorial and Museum of the Holocaust in Los Angeles; to Mrs. Mano, Harbert, who helped to organize the material in this book; to my wife Helen, whose patience and guidance made it possible for me to write this book; to Professor Donald Schwartz of California State University, Long Beach, who helped to edit material and without whose help this book would not have been published; and to all the scholars whose lectures I attended and from whom I learned so much about the horrible times in which I lived.

JOSEPH FREEMAN
Pasadena, California
October 29, 1994

Note About the Publication

In September 1995, I signed an agreement with Paragon House to publish my first book, *Job*. Paragon House forwarded a galley of my book, *Job.*, advising me to look for any errors. I eagerly got to work. In the beginning of October, I received a letter from Paragon informing me that the company was reorganizing and therefore they would suspend the publication of books for a while. I tried to find out how long it would take until they were back in business. Their answer was they didn't know—maybe a year or more. The exact time, they could not tell me.

The company was very nice to me. They gave me two alternatives. One, I could wait until the company started up again and they would publish my book, or two, they would release me from the obligation which I signed with them and I could look for another publishing house.

I contacted Professor John K. Roth and I also asked advise from Nick Street of the editing department of Paragon House. Both of them were of the opinion that *Job* was a good book and would be well received by the public. They both recommended another publisher: The Greenwood Group.

A few years ago at a college in California, I was sharing with students about my life at the death camp. Afterward, I asked the professor, "Did the students read my book, Job?" The answer was "No." The price for the book is $37.98. I didn't write my book to earn money. My purpose was that the generation after the Holocaust could learn what HATE and BIGOTRY can do—destroy. I went to Wromman's Books in Pasadena and I bought a copy of my book for $37.98. It was expensive. I called Professor Roth and discussed what to do. I said, "Well, I have only one solution to try to buy back *Job* from Greenwood Publishing Company. Then find another company which will be willing to publish my book in a paperback edition for less money."

I thought about Paragon House now. I couldn't forget how helpful they initially were. I went back to them and signed a contract to publish Job in a paper back edition. The selling price, $12.95. It's the right price for students.

Contents

Part Three: Rebirth

Maps

Poland on the eve of World War II

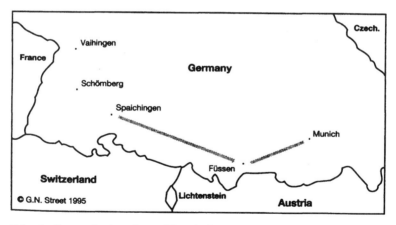

Map indicates the location of Death Camps and the route of the Death March from Spaichingen to Munich, March 16 to April 26, 1945.

Preface

Only as a result of a meeting with Seymour and Rebecca Fromer in 1986 did I consider writing about my experiences during the Holocaust. It is not easy for me to relive the terrors of my past and it is especially difficult to put in black ink on white paper my painful yesteryears.

I met Seymour and Rebecca in 1986 at the Anne Frank Exhibit in the Museum of the Holocaust in Los Angeles. As a docent, I spoke about Anne Frank's life as well as my own, discussing the differences and similarities of our experiences. My talk lasted about a quarter of an hour. Afterwards I spoke with the visitors, at which time Seymour and Rebecca approached me. They asked kindly why I had not written of my experiences, saying my story was unusual and too important to be forgotten. I said I was uncertain, but possibly because I did not have the time or patience.

Their encouragement resulted in my writing this book. It was a difficult process, taking over six years to complete. For the first few weeks, whenever I sat down to write, I could do nothing but cry. The memories of suffering were still so fresh. I needed a little more time to forget.

When at last I began, I wrote for only a few nights at a time, forced to stop and regain my strength. As the past came back to me, often I could not sleep. I would run out of the bedroom to keep my wife, Helen, from seeing what I went through. It was terrifying to relive the moments of pain. Now, I do not know if I would have the patience to do it over.

Yes, finally I finished my life story which will be judged by readers now and by future generations.

Introduction

In the two decades following the end of World War II, very little material was published on the Holocaust. The wound was too raw, the pain too near the surface for survivors to write personal testimonies. The public at large, unwilling to explore and analyze the horrors of the war, was more interested in the process of reconstruction and rehabilitation. The airing of the docudrama "The Holocaust" on television in the 1970s sparked a renewed interest in the subject, as did the movie, *Schindler's List*, which won the Academy Award for Best Picture in 1993.

In recent years there has been a veritable explosion of books and video material related to the Holocaust. At the same time, there has emerged a cadre of pseudoacademicians who insist that the Holocaust was a hoax, that it never happened. It is especially important to counteract these Holocaust deniers, given that many youngsters (and adults) have little understanding of the recent past. Hopefully, the general public will read about the Nazi period from reputable authorities and sources.

No accounts of the Holocaust have been more striking, more compelling than the testimony offered by those who survived the atrocities. From them, readers learn about the emotional dimension of the Holocaust-the shattered relationships, broken dreams, the loss of faith in humanity. Such accounts lend insights not usually gained from more scholarly studies. Unfortunately, the number of firsthand accounts is limited; this invaluable resource is dwindling as the numbers of survivors decrease with each passing year.

It is for this reason that Joseph Freeman's personal narrative is a treasure. He writes movingly of unimaginable horrors at the hands of the Nazis and of his emotional reactions to unspeakable crimes. A deeply religious man, he questions the reasons for his suffering; he is a modern-day Job whose faith is severely tested. His story represents the triumph of determination, a testament of the will to survive. But it also bears witness to the emotional price paid by a survivor and the impact on his family relationships in the decades that followed. In an attempt to avoid feeling the pain of his past, Joseph Freeman spent the years after 1945 working feverishly in business, engrossed in the effort to rebuild life for himself and for his family.

But the past would not die and Joseph recognized he would have to come to grips with his awful experiences. Late in life he decided to go back to school to study the period he lived through. He devoted the next twelve years to reading about the Holocaust and working with scholars on that subject. At last, Joseph Freeman felt he had come to terms with the Holocaust, and he has dedicated the rest of his life to teaching others about the victimization of European Jewry during the Nazi era.

This book represents the culmination of that effort.

DONALD SCHWARTZ
History Department
California State University, Long Beach

PART ONE

Before the Destruction

In the Land of Uz there lived a man whose name was Job. This man was blameless and upright; he feared God and shunned evil.

The Beginning.

Job, Prologue, Verse 1

Chapter One

Early School Years in Radom

I was born in the city of Radom, which is located in the center of Poland. My father was in the leather business most of his life, this having been our family trade for generations. He also made money in real estate and we were wealthy or, at least, middle class. As I recall my youth, I had everything a child could dream of.

When I was three my parents sent me to *cheder*, or religious school, where I learned to read Torah, interpretations of Torah, and to pray in Hebrew. The first day the rabbi asked my mother why she had brought a girl. "This school is for boys only," he said, then told her to have my hair cut. Even now I can feel the tears running down my cheeks at the barbers.

Every Saturday after dinner, I went to my maternal grandfather's house to be tested on my studies. On this side of my family there were several rabbis. My great grandfather, Israel Gutman, was a rabbi in our city. His son, my grandfather's brother, Rachmil Gutman, was a rabbi in the city of Kishenov. I remember Rachmil sitting with my grandfather at the living room table, my father standing to their side, and I, standing in front of them with the Torah, being tested. I read a few verses, then read the interpretation, Rashi. If I read correctly, Rachmil turned to my grandfather, nodded his head, and I got an apple. If not, my grandfather turned to my father and asked in a loud voice, "What has he been doing all week?"

In our Jewish community, parents worked very hard to give their children the opportunity to learn, to gain knowledge. Knowledge is one thing that can never be taken away. We have been the people of the book. In this way, we Jews survived the thousands of years living in Diaspora.

As a result of the hatred the Polish people felt for Jews while I was growing up, I always had a fear of something happening to me or someone in my family. As a precautionary measure, whenever going to *cheder* at night, I waited to be joined by other boys. Though we walked in groups and carried hand lanterns—as there was as yet no electricity for streetlights—we were fearful of attacks from Polish boys. At Christmastime, Jews stayed far from churches as Poles used the occasion to accuse Jews of deicide and to kill them.

Soon after the independence of Poland in 1919, there were many pogroms. I remember the name of the pogrom leader, Petliura. Relatives who came to our home to escape from him and his hordes told us stories so terrible that I was afraid to sleep at night.

This was the atmosphere in which my generation grew up.

From the time when I turned seven until I was fourteen, my parents sent me to a public school where I learned the Polish and German languages. In 1928 when I turned thirteen, I had my bar mitzvah, the first of my grandparents' grandsons to have one. My brothers, Elek and Isaac, who were both older than I, did not. Elek was physically disabled and ill, and Isaac ran away from *cheder* and, as a result, never prepared for his bar mitzvah.

My father invited guests to the shul for the celebration. When I was called up to read the Torah portion of the week and the Haftorah, my father stood beside me, listening as I chanted the melody it took me months to learn. As I turned around to be blessed by the rabbi, I saw tears in my father's eyes. He nodded at me and I knew then that he was happy, that he was proud of me.

My grandmother made challah and a special kind of fish for everyone in the shul; my father ordered a very expensive Carmel wine from the Holy Land. There was singing and dancing, and afterwards my parents, Isaac, Elek, my younger sister, Tania, and the rest of my family went to my grandparents' house. There my grandmother presented me with a gift wrapped in gold paper—a savings book showing a deposit of seventy-two *zloty*, or four times eighteen. Eighteen was a symbol of luck. In Hebrew it represents life.

I spent much of my childhood reading rather than playing outside. Radom's librarians knew me well and often reserved recently published books for me. With an excellent memory, I was able to speak and to write about the books I read and to reduce the time needed to do homework. Whenever I had a few minutes free I would read. At night when everyone was asleep I read until very late, a candle in one hand and a book in the other.

Chapter Two

Father's Family in Staszow

The happiest season for me was summer. No school! During these vacation days, my father and I traveled four hours by bus on unpaved roads to my grandfather's house in the city of Staszow. Poland, a new country having gained its independence only a few years earlier, was very poor and our only means of transportation were by horse and buggy or bus. The bus was both slow and costly.

In this little city in Poland, the Freemans lived for hundreds of years in peace with little disturbance. But when the Germans came in 1939, at the time of World War II, many Poles collaborated with the Nazis. We have to understand what happened in Poland not so long ago. The Nazis in November of 1939 rounded up and liquidated the leaders and the intellectual class of the Polish nation, which totaled about 650,000 people. The Polish nation was left without leaders. The Nazis knew the hate which had existed for years. The Poles collaborated with the Nazis in all matters having to do with the Jewish people. This was what many of them had been waiting for, to get rid of the Jews. This anti-Semitic battle with the Jews had been going on before the war. Now since the destruction of Poland by the Nazis, the way was opened to destroy the Jewish people in this conquered country. Yes, there were a few whose moral fiber was strong and they did save some Jewish lives, but not too many. From my own experience in our family, a young

Polish woman from the city of Staszow saved nine members of the Freeman family. Steve, one of my uncles, married the woman who saved him and the members of our family.

At that moment they were living happily in this country. Still, in the western part of Europe, more people of the Christian faith had been helping our people to survive. We call them Righteous Gentiles and they have a special place in the Holocaust Museum in Jerusalem, never to be forgotten. It was easy for the Nazis to exterminate our people, knowing that the Poles would not help our people to escape. For a mere one pound of butter or a salami, the Poles gave Jews to the Germans to be killed.

But now let's get back to my life—the life of a generation that went through hell. Only a few of us survived the terrible experience to be able to share it.

My grandfather owned a tannery and nearly all of the houses in the city of Staszow, which was under Russian occupation from 1792 to 1918. Also very learned in the Torah, he rose early and went to shul to pray, came home a few hours later, breakfasted on a roll and a glass of milk, returned to shul to meditate until two o'clock in the afternoon, then he stayed at his business until the five o'clock closing. He then came home for dinner, which my grandmother prepared, then returned to shul to study Talmud until midnight. Studying Talmud was the most important activity in my grandfather's life, and it was my grandmother who primarily took care of the business. Counting the Polish maids, our home included thirteen children. Six of the children were from my grandfather's first wife, who was the sister of his second wife. She had died young, and his second marriage had taken place according to the Torah; "When a man's wife dies, leaving behind children, if she has a sister, he is to marry her. Thus his second wife was both my step grandmother as well as my great-aunt. She was a wise woman, educated, skilled in business, and good with the family. My father went to the yeshiva until he was sixteen, then he joined the family business, until 1910 when he married and moved from Staszow to Radom.

I vividly recall the moment when my father, my grandfather, and my uncles went to the little shul in the city of Staszow. This was the evening when my grandfather would say Kaddish in the memory of his first wife, my grandmother. After the service the community relived an unusual event, a parade of the Freeman family clan. First, my grandfather left the place of prayers, then my father followed a few steps behind, then Uncle Symon and Uncle Jacob followed behind my father. They came from Warsaw to be together with the family on this occasion. At the end of the parade I walked—the grandson. I was always going with my father on this unusual occasion. My grandfather held a little pad in his hands full of half *zlotys* (fifty cents in American money). The poor people of the city had been waiting a whole year to get this little bit of money from my grandfather. He moved slowly, giving to the poor people a few half-*zloty*. Remember that in Poland at the beginning of the twentieth century, ninety percent of the Jewish population was very poor. The Jewish community in Poland was able to survive thanks to the Jewish community in America, which lent financial support.

This was the tradition in the Jewish way of life. The rich, the fortunate ones, gave to Charitas Tzedaka so that the poor could go on living. This is the way we Jewish people lived, by helping each other. I always look at my family with pride wherever they lived, for the support and active part they took in the lives of the Jewish community. This I learned from my father. My family and I follow the tradition. After the war wherever I lived, I supported charities and institutions as I did when I lived in Germany; I have continued to do so ever since I came to this country.

One of my dearest memories is of Sunday afternoons at my grandparents' house. My grandfather meditating over the Talmud and my grandmother sitting in the rocking chair. My father, with my Uncles Symon and Jacob played cards, and two of my other uncles played music—Elias at the piano and Steve on the violin. I stood to the side, their audience. If I made any noise, my grandfather would turn around and put his finger in front of his mouth, making a sign for me to be silent and then he would smile at me.

I remember too the days my grandfather came to Radom to buy merchandise to be sold in Staszow for the holidays. At this time the ghetto had been recently opened and Jews were mixing freely in Polish society. My family was one of those developing a thriving business as a result of freedom of commerce. My father became quite wealthy with his two brothers, Symon and Jacob, running the wholesale leather stores in Radom and Warsaw, as well as a larger network of stores throughout Poland. In 1928, my father, along with my two uncles, built a house for themselves. Not long afterwards, my two uncles purchased a 300-unit apartment complex in Warsaw into which they moved.

Whenever my grandfather stayed at our home, he was given a great deal of respect. One of the occasions when he was with us was *Tishak-b'Ab*, the holiday commemorating the destruction of the holy temples in Jerusalem. Already fast asleep, I was awakened at midnight by the sound of his chanting. I climbed out of bed and stood watching him through a crack in my door as he sat on a low chair—a symbol of mourning—shoes removed, with a candle in one hand and a *siddur* in the other, chanting the prayer *Tikkun Chacot* in a special melody, and crying. I stood, afraid to move, shaking as I listened to the prayers of my grandfather. Then I turned, climbed back in bed, and pulled the covers over my head. Though very tired, it took me a long time to fall back asleep. The next morning when I asked my father about my grandfather's unusual behavior, he explained the holiday.

These memories of my home, my family, and my tradition will always remain with me though their reality no longer exists, having been destroyed by the Nazis.

Chapter Three

Gymnasium and University Years

When I was fourteen I entered gymnasium in Radom and there continued my enthusiasm for studying. In 1930, at the age of fifteen, I joined a Zionist group, attending a leadership training camp in the summer.

In 1934, I received my degree in Hebrew Literature. My examiner, Professor Tartakower from the University in Lodz, was an internationally known figure in the field of Jewish history. I carefully studied the several books he wrote on the history of the Jews in Poland. My exam topic was Job, and for one hour I spoke in biblical Hebrew on the subject. History was my passion, yet my mother said I could not make a living as an historian. I could always make a living as a doctor or dentist, and so my parents supported me under the condition that I study medicine.

It was very difficult for Jews to get into the universities, particularly in the fields of medicine and dentistry. My Uncle Elias, who was an exceptionally bright student in gymnasium, was able to enroll in the University of Krakow, then transfer to the University of Warsaw only through the connections of my Uncle Jacob. My Uncle Steve, who had been an officer in the Polish army, was accepted to study dentistry, only as a result of his service.

Upon graduating gymnasium with honors in 1935, I was

sent by my parents to a private university in Warsaw, Wolna Wszechnica Polska, the Polish Freedom Place for Learning. During my time at the university I was not required to take final exams, as the professors knew my abilities. Often I was the first to respond to a professor's request to have a student summarize the lecture, and I was called up in front to the blackboard. I hungered for knowledge. I bent to my parents' will and studied medicine, though often without their being aware, I went to history lectures in order to gain intellectual nourishment.

During this time, in 1936, I became involved in leading Zionist activities at the University's Student Circle under the supervision of Menachem Begin. Demanding rights as Jews and as citizens of Poland, we fought with Polish students in order to be allowed to study, at times having to struggle to enter the lecture halls.

In that same year, in the town of Przytyk, a pogrom occurred. Those Jews who attempted to defend themselves against the killings were thrown in jail by the Polish police. This was Poland shortly before World War II. The Nazis were to remember this when they occupied Poland, and later used the hate which was burning so deep in the Polish soul as a tool to destroy us.

Many changes were occurring in Poland, and when my cousin Julius and I were ready to enter medical programs at the university, my Uncle Jacob's connections would no longer help. We were told we would have to wait. Julius went to Belgium to study while I stayed in Radom, studied French, and prepared to follow him.

PART TWO

Hashoah

One day the angels came to present themselves before the LORD, and Satan also came with them. The LORD said to Satan, "Where have you come from?"

Satan answered the LORD, "From roaming through the earth and going to and from in it."

Then the LORD said to Satan, "Have you considered my servant Job? There is no-one on earth like him; he is blameless and upright, a man who fears God and shuns evil."

"Does Job fear God for nothing?" Satan replied, "Have you not put a hedge around him and his household and everything   he has? You have blessed the work of his hands, so that his flocks and herds are spread throughout the land. But stretch out your hand and strike everything he has, and he will surely curse you to your face."

The LORD said to Satan, "Very well, then, everything he has is in your hands, but on the man himself do not lay a finger"

Then Satan went out from the presence of the LORD.

JOB, PROLOGUE, VERSES 6 TO 12

Chapter Four

September 1, 1939

September 1, 1939. World War II. So many years ago. The memories are still with me. The falling bombs, the houses coming apart, the crying and calling for help from those caught in the ruins, the low-flying German airplanes, the trembling of the earth beneath my feet.

At our house at 34 Zeromskiego Street, we received orders on the radio to dig ditches for protection from the bombing. All young men were directed to travel to the opposite side of the Bug River, close to the Russian border. Approximately 300 miles away, we were to build up an army to push the Germans back and thereby free Poland. At that moment we were unaware of the might of the German war machine, and in particular, of its air force. The Germans left Poland in ruins in only a few weeks. The civilian population was slaughtered. Tens of thousands were killed on the highways when, according to government orders, they ran from their homes. The confusion, the traffic jams, all of it is too terrible to describe.

In running to Kovno, my brother Isaac, my uncles Aaron and Elias, and I, became separated. My brother and I stayed in Kovno where we met my maternal uncle Szlamek. Within a few weeks we became ill and returned to Radom. The night we reached the Bug River, a German soldier in his early sixties forced us to pay money to cross and asked why we were returning. "Don't go back," he said. "There is no place for Jews in a

Nazi-occupied territory." We did not believe him. How could we? How could anyone believe the Nazis would do what they did? I often wonder how I survived the hell I went through during the six years that followed.

We came back to the City of Radom.

Our home was now shared by my parents with a German soldier. Under orders from the Nazis, they had turned over a large portion of our house. These orders were being enforced all over Poland. In a short time we, as well as all other Jews in expensive homes, were forced out entirely.

Fortunately for us, we moved to the Zamlynia Street estate of the Eismans, whom my father knew. In October I began work in the St. Kazimierza Hospital's bacteriology laboratory. Also employed in the laboratory were Pola Reich, Sala Zlotnik, and Mania Milstein, friends of mine. My close friend Gimpel Weintraub, with whom I attended public school and gymnasium, worked in the medical department.

One day as I walked with my friends down the main corridor, I passed the hospital director who was walking with a German doctor. The doctor came in to operate on a German soldier wounded in the conquest of Poland. He looked at us, then turned to the director and asked, *"Was machen die Juden hier?"* ("What are the Jews doing here?").

I knew very well what to expect. Dr. Witkowsky, the director, called us into his office and told us we must leave the hospital. He said he had no choice in the matter. Jews could not work in the hospital as they were prohibited by Nazi law from taking care of non-Jewish people. This was the first time at work that I encountered the Nuremberg Laws and, though I found it hard to understand, this was the new order of the Nazi Paradise. It was also the last time I worked outside of the ghetto.

The Germans moved Jews from one part of the city to another until they formed a ghetto. I began to work in the ghetto under the supervision of Professor Worcman. Schools for Jewish children had been shut down under Nazi directives, so we taught our children at night. However, the activity soon became too dangerous and we stopped.

Chapter Five

Walowa Street Ghetto

In the beginning of 1941, my family moved from the Eisman estate to a small house at 20 Walowa Street in the Walowa Street ghetto established by the Germans. Over twenty thousand Jews now lived there. The second ghetto, centered around Glinice Street, was smaller. My mother had chosen a small house as she felt it would be easier for us to get through the crisis living "in the shade," not showing our presence much in the ghetto, not being constantly in the eyes of others, our names on the lips of others. We believed the Nazis when they told us that we would be working for the army, and our families would be taken care of by them. We believed until the last minute.

After my work with Professor Worcman ended, I worked for the typhus department with an assistant, Eisenberg, transporting by horse and wagon those in the ghetto infected with typhus. Under orders, we first transported the sick to the ambulatorium, a shul converted by the Germans for collection of the sick, where we left them for a few days until, in the mornings around eight o'clock, we transported them to the hospital quarantine outside the ghetto. En route, we drove fast without stopping, as we were ordered, and the German police, knowing our route, did not stop us. The hospital, on Warszawska Street, was two kilometers away and stood across from the Koszary, where the 72nd Brigade of the Polish army had been stationed before the war.

Once, when I was not well, my assistant transported the sick to the hospital. On the way back he stopped to buy meat from someone who was Polish. In the wagon, he put the meat under the seat and covered it with a blanket. At the gate of the ghetto, the SS were waiting for him. They pulled him out of the wagon, took the meat out from under the seat, placed it on the ground, and told him to pick it up. As he bent down, they shot him. They then ordered Jewish police to bring a sack, put the meat and the body inside of it, and take it to Pentz Garden for burial.

That ended my job. I then worked for the disinfection department, in charge of a sulfur warehouse for disinfection of the houses in the ghetto. The SS had ordered the Jewish police to disinfect the ghetto with sulfur, block by block. On a typical day, the Jewish police and our disinfection department workers ordered residents to move out by eight o'clock the next morning. In the intervening time, the rich came to pay the police in order to avoid the process. The police then sent them to our department where I collected the money—forty *zloty* per apartment—with my assistant, a boy named Mietek Wiszlicky. Each block took us about four hours, as we placed pads of sulfur in the homes and, at the end of the process, returned to remove them. As we worked, I gave the head of the typhus department, Gimpel Weintraub, the names of the rich as well and their payment which he divided among the three of us, the police, and Dr. Szenderowicz, the hospital director. In order to make extra money, over the next few months of my work I accumulated 4,000 pounds of sulfur and sold it to Polish citizens. Money, as long as we were in Radom, opened doors.

One night in the summer of 1941, after we were already asleep, the Polish police and the SS came to my family's home.

We were awakened by their knocking, the force of which was frightening. They asked for me by name. When I identified myself, they dragged me from the apartment and took me out of the ghetto to the police station on Peretza Street. I sat in a closed room at the station for three nights, afraid to sleep as it was well known that if the SS took someone away, that person was lost. Yet my mother suffered more than I. I was her favorite son.

Some Jews who felt it would save them by collaborating had reported the wealth of my family to the police. After the first day of my imprisonment, my parents found out they would be required to pay the police a ransom of 50,000 *zloty*.

In January 1940, the Nazis ordered Jews to register their property—all factories, business enterprises, workshops, and houses. Any goods and valuables found in homes and in warehouses were also confiscated. My father managed to hide a roomful of leather, which he quickly sold for quite a bit of money, exchanging the *zloty* for gold and foreign currency. Over the next year, he liquidated what remained at the tannery in Radom. He placed the money from the sales inside metal boxes and glass jars and buried them in various spots on our properties, showing the locations to my brother Isaac and me. My father used some money to pay ransom for me. I was very lucky. This time the money saved me.

Upon my release I did not go back to my job, but stayed home. The situation in the ghetto worsened, with Germans increasingly restricting the movements of Jews. Jews were no longer allowed to go to work without being escorted by the Jewish police and the SS.

With money it was possible to gain work that was not too difficult. The Jewish police and individuals in the *Arbeitsamt* (employment office) knew which jobs were easier and would secure them for a price. After a while my father was able to arrange to pay a large sum of money in exchange for a position for me at the Kromolowsky Place factory. At the time, I did not know that working at the factory would save me from being sent to the extermination camp at the time of liquidation of the ghetto in our city.

At first we went to work every morning, spending the day repairing saddles and leather goods for the German army. In the evening we went back to the ghetto with a Jewish police escort. Shortly, however, orders came for us to bring bedding to the factory, to sleep on the premises, and return to our homes in the ghetto only on Sundays.

While our conditions became ever more restrictive, the ghetto became a horror. The SS came to the ghetto and took Jews away. Those Jews were never seen again. The SS shot the sick; they shot the elderly. List in hand; the SS killed Jews before their families' eyes.

On Sundays, returning to the ghetto, we saw people who lay sick, hungry, crying, begging for help on the sidewalks. As the SS entered, people rushed to hide in their cellars.

During all of this we continued to live at 20 Walowa Street.

Chapter Six

How the City of Radom Died

AUGUST 16, 1942.

I remember how our city died, a city of 35,000 Jewish people. The Nazis began their slaughter. This horrible picture is still before my eyes. It was more than fifty years ago, but still I think of it as if it happened yesterday or maybe a few hours ago.

The part of Poland in which we lived was beautiful in the summer. There was never any rain, not even clouds. It was morning, early. The first rays of the sun shone on the horizon. The streetlights were still on, beaming across the ghetto. The city was quiet as people were still half-asleep. The weather was warm. It remained quiet and then, suddenly, at five o'clock, the SS and the Polish police by the hundreds came into the ghetto. They moved from house to house, pounding on the doors with long metal bars, and forcing residents out of their homes, chasing them down the streets, beating them with sticks and instruments. The SS directed the flow of the crowds to the marketplace.

In my home, as we watched from the window, the SS and the Polish police approached. The noise grew ever louder and louder. People were calling to each other and crying. There was running on the steps below, then pounding on our door with metal bars. The SS broke it wide open, yelling, *Schnell raus!* ("Out quickly!"). The SS hit us on our heads, throwing us from the room. One of the SS men shouted, "*Macht schnell!*" ("Move quickly!"). They beat us, shoving us down the steps. My parents went first. Behind them, my brother Isaac and I pulled along our disabled brother, Elek, with our sister, Tania, behind us.

The SS followed. We were moving fast, running down the steps, then out of the house. Once outside amongst a throng of thousands, we saw the horror of people lying on the ground, some dead, some still writhing, blood running from their wounds. Children ran and screamed, "Mother, mother . . ." yet no one responded. Everywhere people were praying. The SS chased us with dogs, constantly pushing and hitting, shoving us toward the marketplace. Shots resounded through the streets. The sick, the elderly, the slow, were killed, at times kicked to death by the SS, who smiled even as they did this. One of the SS held a bottle of vodka as he shot our people. Old men in prayer shawls knelt, saying their final prayers as the SS stood behind them with revolvers, and shot.

While some of us were chased, others were pushed into a large group. My family was shoved into this group, packed closer and closer, as more people were added. There we saw the SS throwing small children out of second and third-story windows. Some survived and lay crying on the ground, and these the SS stepped on with their boots, smashing their heads. The women who tried to protect their children were shot. In horror we watched the crying, the bursts of machine guns, the bodies falling to the ground. We heard the prayer *Shema Yisrael* on the lips of the dying. Before my eyes, many, many of my friends and relatives were killed.

So many dead. Bodies were all around us. After a while, the SS and the Polish police gathered the dead into a single place, a growing mountain of bodies. Some of the dying but still alive were among them. These people were shot in the head. Still the SS ran after the others, beating them to make them run faster. The slow ones were shot in place.

For hours, the SS and the Polish police rounded up the Jews. All six members of my family stood together—my mother and father, my sister and my two brothers, and I—frozen to the spot, wide-eyed, crying, and shaking. The SS, like hunters, went through our ranks and pulled people out. The old and weak were put to one side, the young and strong to the other. As one of the SS passed my family he pulled my mother out and threw her to the side of the weak, away from us. This moment is very painful to relive, this moment of tragedy which touched me so deeply. I can still see my mother's lovely face, crying, as she was pushed away from us. Over and over again, she called my name. Her voice calling *Joseph, Joseph* still rings in my ears.

As she stood about twenty feet away from us, I do not know even now what came over me, but I turned to my sister and handed her a bundle of dollar bills. "Tania," I said, "go to mother and stay with her. Help her. We'll join you in a few weeks."

The Germans said they were sending people to the east to work for the army, claiming they needed more manpower. I did not realize this was the last time I would ever speak to my sister. She was so young, only twenty-one, and so beautiful. She went over to our mother, put her arms around her, and helped her turn to see where I was. My father stood beside me, praying. Neither of us knew if we would be killed just for being witnesses to this slaughter. The SS with their dogs and the Polish police shoved my mother and sister toward the railroad station, from which they would leave the ghetto. As Tania held our mother, her face was filled with tears and she cried aloud. My mother raised her hand high and waved good-bye. This was the last moment I saw my mother and my sister. It all happened too quickly.

They both went to their deaths. I did not know I was sending my younger sister to her death. Since then, I sometimes awake during the night, shaking. For as long as I live, I will not forget that I sent Tama away, and I cannot forgive myself for it. She was in line to stay and to work, and though she may not have survived even so, I feel to blame for her death. She could have lived for a while at least.

Chapter Seven

Selections for the Death Camps

The selecting and killing went on for hours. Meanwhile, the SS took approximately one hundred young men from our group and put them to work collecting the dead strewn everywhere in pools of blood, dragging them to horse wagons, piling them on top of each other. Wagons full of bodies were driven from the ghetto and buried in a large ditch at Pentz Garden. In 1945, I visited the graveyard and said Kaddish in their memory.

We stood for hours in the middle of the marketplace, the leftovers, the temporary survivors of the community. Some of us passed out from hunger and exhaustion. The rest of us prayed, looking to the sky. Based on what we had seen that day, we believed there was no chance for our survival. And we ceased to care what would happen next. Those who passed out were pulled from the group and killed there in front of us. We wondered if we would be next.

At 5:30 in the evening, the SS told those who remained to go back home. We dragged my crippled brother and went upstairs to our apartment, tired, hungry, shocked, and unable to think of what to do. Crying and hugging each other, we had no words. Each time we started to talk, it turned to tears. My father took Elek to a chair, gave him some water, and tried to comfort him. My brother held his hand and looked up at him. Then my father placed him on the bed and gave him a piece of challah, telling him to eat.

I could not think clearly. I could not believe what I had been a witness to. I was still in shock. I just looked around with my eyes wide open. As my father turned to my brother and me, his look was unforgettable. Tears filled his eyes. He raised his hands high above his head and asked, "What can I do for my children to protect them?" And he started to cry aloud.

I walked over to him and put my arms around him. I cried. I sobbed. After a while I asked him to come with me to my workplace. My brother Isaac and I received *Arbeitscheine* (a temporary labor card) to go back to work. I repeatedly asked my father to go with me as I had the opportunity to take someone, though Isaac did not. I felt my father would have a better chance at survival if he were with me.

My crippled brother, Elek, sat on the bed, looking at my father and me. He started to cry, his voice trembling as he said to our father, "Dad, you are my father. I am your son. Joseph is your son too, but he is young and strong. He can help himself. Your place is with me." He sobbed, choking on his tears. My father put his arms around him, and then turned to me with these words, "Joseph, you and Elek are both my sons, but you are strong and he is disabled. Go to your workplace. Save yourself. I cannot go with you. My place is with him and this is my final choice. I will share the faith with him."

Still I tried to persuade him. He refused to listen. He said, "Joseph, go before they come back for us. We may be next."

As he gave me a rolled-up Persian rug from behind the bed, he said, "May the Lord take care of you," hugging and kissing me. He blessed me, his hands on top of my head.

I looked at my father one last time as he sat down. Then I kissed him, shook hands with Elek, and turned and said good-bye to Isaac, who had been silently watching us. Going down the steps to the street, I cried. If I had waited one more minute, I could not have left them. This was the last time I saw my father and my two brothers.

The streets were deserted and silent. Not a soul moved. Now, at eleven o'clock at night, no sign remained of what had happened during the day. I moved to the dark side of the street. Several policemen passed and I hid, bent over, behind the houses.

Running down the streets, from one house to another, I heard people praying and crying. The voices followed me wherever I went. At last I arrived at Pentz Garden, jumped through the fence, and was out of the ghetto. To reach the factory where I worked, I walked through the fields for four hours. When I arrived, I was drenched in sweat and could not move another inch. I rested. People asked me what had happened in the city. Exhausted, I could not talk.

I went to my workroom, dropped onto the bed, and sobbed. When the morning came, I was still in shock and, though I felt sick, I went to work, cleaning the factory.

A few days later a friend, a policeman in the ghetto, came to tell me that the day after the selection the SS had returned. The weak and old, who were on one side, were taken to Pentz Garden and shot in the head. Those children who had somehow survived the previous day's massacre were killed on the spot. Those found trying to hide were also killed. The SS, the Polish police, and some young men piled the dead in one location.

My friend had seen my father and Elek. Elek, hiding behind my father and clutching his hand, was grabbed by one of the SS and killed before my father's eyes. My friend told me that my father bent over Elek, kissed him, said Kaddish, then something came over my father and he tried to jump a fence. As a Polish policeman grabbed him, one of the SS approached and shot my father. Still he held on to the fence. The police pulled him down. They dragged him away. Where they buried my father, my friend did not know.

And so in a very short time I lost my lovely mother, my father, my brother Elek, and my sister. I knew nothing of what happened to Isaac.

For two weeks each night I cried until the morning came. I relived the departure of my mother and sister and what I heard of the killing of my father and brother.

Slowly I absorbed what had happened to me.

Chapter Eight
Kromolowsky Factory

During the next few months I lived and worked at Kromolowsky, the factory for repairing leather goods and saddles for the army and the SS. I worked with approximately one hundred and fifty others, most of who were wealthy and had come to Kromolowsky prior to the liquidation on August 16, bringing their personal belongings and quite a bit of money.

Our supervisor, who was a *Volksdeutsch* (a German living outside Germany), liked to have vodka, money, and gifts for his family. So we paid to keep him satisfied and, in exchange, worked less. Our schedule was not strict except when orders came in from the *Wehrmacht* and the SS. These had to be sent out on time. Often we paid our two foremen to fill some of the orders, and those among us who were too sick or too old to work paid poor residents from the ghetto as replacements. A Jewish policeman, a gentle soul by the name of Kampel, escorted workers from the ghetto to Kromolowsky in the morning and back home in the evening. He was our connection to the ghetto.

Our factory building, approximately 150 by 80 feet, stood across from another, smaller building in which I had my sleeping quarters. There I kept a small wooden bed, a few blankets, and the carpet my father gave me. Beside this building there was an even smaller building in which we prepared our food.

The head of Kromolowsky was a German army major who lived in the city of Radom. Each morning after being driven to the factory, he stepped from the car and conducted a surveillance of the outside of the factory, calling for me immediately as I was the one who kept the premises clean, in addition to working as an assistant to the electrician. "Joseph, are you happy with your work?" was his first question, followed by a series of others as I accompanied him. After ten minutes he left me and went into his office, a room separate from the factory. Not once did he enter the factory, but rather left that task to our supervisor, the *Volksdeutsch*.

Many of the workers, primarily the families, lived on the second floor of the factory, a single large room divided into small rooms by hanging blankets. Inside most of these rooms there were beds on both sides, bookshelves, and a small table in the middle, furniture made by the factory's carpenter in exchange for money. They brought with them bedding and other possessions when they fled their homes. In the large communal area, tables and benches were set up, and it was here that everyone sat after work, eating, talking, and trying not to think about tomorrow.

Each morning at around 8:30, we had a cup of coffee and a piece of bread, at times even a bit of preserves. When the whistle blew we were at the workplace to receive orders for the day from the *Volksdeutsch*. Once the orders were given, the *Volksdeutsch* left and the foreman took over, watching to see that the orders were filled properly. After an hour or so, Policeman Kampel escorted in workers from the ghetto. From 12:30 to 1:00 we stopped for lunch, again a cup of coffee and a piece of bread. The whistle blew and we were back at work, continuing until the last whistle at 4:30, the end of our workday.

Kitchen workers, women from our group, prepared our meals during the day, and dinner usually consisted of a soup of reasonable quality. Though it was possible to get by on this diet, some looked for something better to eat and thus turned to me, knowing that in the ghetto I had always managed to obtain food.

At this moment in writing, I am overwhelmed, filled with memories of when I arrived at Kromolowsky after the liquidation. It was terrifying for me as I lay on my bed reliving what happened, seeing again the SS beat my mother, her lovely face covered with blood. Tania's arm around her as they walked away crying and calling for help that never came. Their voices rang in my ears. Elek's voice was with me. I spent countless sleepless nights; it took weeks to understand that my life was continuing and that I had to somehow make peace with the loss of my family.

I cannot write anymore. I have to stop for a while. My eyes are blurred with tears. Remember what I share with you—my painful memories of the past. Maybe in sharing them with me you will realize and understand what bigotry and hatred can do.

Chapter Nine

Business at Kromolowsky

Knowing that in the ghetto I found ways to obtain food, a quite wealthy man by the name of Mr. Richtman approached me and asked if I could buy food for him and others, saying I would be paid for doing so. I told him I would think it over and see if it were possible without risking my life.

I decided I had to speak with a *Volksdeutsch* named Minsky who was gatekeeper in the small building at the factory's entrance. As of yet, I had taken no money from Richtman, not wanting to be accused of cheating him should anything go wrong. I approached Minsky the next evening with the idea of selling my carpet, worth 4,000 *zloty*. Talking with him, I began to feel we could do business, but that I would have to be very careful. When I asked if he would be interested in buying this very beautiful and valuable carpet I had, he said I should bring it in for him to look at.

I will never forget the moment I returned to my sleeping quarters and took my carpet from under my bed. It was the carpet my mother bought when my father built our family home on Zeromskiego Street in 1928. Tears swelled in my eyes recalling the moment my father gave it to me, just several hours before he was killed by the SS.

Back at the gatekeeper's station, I unrolled the carpet in front of Minsky. I knew he liked it, and when he asked the price, I told him 2,000 *zloty*. Immediately, he took the money from his pocket and paid me. I knew then that the way was open to do business.

I went back to my room, thinking how I could ask him to help me buy food. Though I was still afraid, I felt he would not report me to the supervisor, given that I could, in turn, expose his having bought the carpet from me.

It took a lot of courage to go to him the next evening and ask him to help me buy food. I said I would pay him. He said he needed time to think it over. A few days passed. I went to his station again. His answer was yes, but he warned me I would have to be very careful not to be caught by the Germans. Later that evening I spoke with Richtman to tell him to have the money ready.

The next evening I returned to see Minsky. I paid him for the basket of food he had ready and took the food back to my room, where I divided it into small packages, then brought them to Richtman. This was the first time I made money selling food.

The following evening I returned to Minsky with a small cart. He informed me he had to remain at his post, but introduced me to a few Polish people who he said were good people, trustworthy, and would help me. Naturally, he said, I had to pay for their assistance. I agreed to do so, put my armband with the Star of David in my pocket and went with them. I was too young to realize the danger I was putting myself in, to realize I was playing with my life. I only thought of how to get food for the others and make money for myself.

The Polish people took me to a place not far from the factory, a small house where food was already waiting for me: two pieces of smoked meat, two loaves of bread, two bottles of fresh cream, three fresh cheeses, and a roasted chicken. Without discussion of price, I paid what they asked.

Pulling my little cart full of food, I returned to Minsky, paid him fifty *zloty*, then went to my room, as I had the night before divided the food into small packages, and brought them to Richtman. That night there were people waiting in his room to buy food. Shortly I sold all of it. I made my first 400 *zloty* profit and I had some free food, too. Happy to have a means to earn money, exhausted from all the activity, I returned to my room. I quickly fell asleep.

Chapter Ten

Isaac

Polish people often came to the factory and talked with us. At times, out of sight of the supervisor, behind the building or in the restrooms, they sold clothes to us. To ensure they would not run off with our money, we had the merchandise in hand before paying. Once I began selling food, I could afford to buy nice clothes and, in general, I began to relax a little. Though at night as I lay in bed, terrible memories still haunted me.

My brain worked constantly on the problem of how to go on living and not fear the living hell—the death, the human devils—the SS I had seen during the liquidation of the ghetto. Something told me not to lose hope, that as long as I was alive there was hope, and that nothing lasted forever. Often when I lay in bed with these thoughts, I wondered where my brother Isaac might be. I had tried to communicate with his workplace, the *Waffen* (war) factory, but failed.

Eventually, I decided the only way to reach my brother was through Kampel, the Jewish police escort for workers from the ghetto. I approached him, taking quite a chance by doing so, and said how much I appreciated his bringing me news of my father and Elek—that no one else had done so. I asked if he knew what happened to Isaac? (I believe he had known him personally). He heard that my brother was supposed to be at the *Waffen* factory. I asked if it would be possible to find out for certain. He said he would try. After a few days of waiting, I feared the news that Isaac had perished too, and I began to want to delay the moment when I would know for certain. In the end, I went back to Kampel. He said information about my brother would cost me money. When I asked how much, he said 200 *zloty*. I agreed to pay.

At last, a few days later, Kampel brought a letter from Isaac, which I quickly took to my room, opened, and read. My brother was alive! I was not alone anymore. My eyes were blurred with tears. That letter I read over and over. In it, Isaac said that he was working at Obsada, making parts for guns, that the work was very difficult, and he wanted to know if I could send money for him to pay to be transferred. Many people at the factory had managed to get transferred by paying the foreman.

I immediately spoke to Kampel. He said I would have to pay if I wanted to send Isaac money, 400 *zloty*. I paid him his money and gave him 1,000 *zloty* plus a letter to my brother. In a few days, I received a letter back in which Isaac thanked me and let me know he had been transferred. I cried. Holding tightly to the letter, I thanked God for allowing me to help my brother. That night as I lay in my bed, I thought of how good it was to be alive. I was not alone anymore. I had someone to take care of.

As I continued my business with Minsky, I was able to send Isaac money every week. Then one Sunday he visited. It was a very happy moment. We sat and talked and we cried. We spoke of our father, of his decision to stay with Elek, and of his words, "Go to your workplace. Save yourself." Isaac told me that during their last moments together, our father blessed him and pushed him toward the door. "The Lord will take care of you" were his parting words. I then repeated to Isaac what Kampel had seen, the killing of Elek and our father.

At last I said to him, "We are alive, the two sole survivors of the Freeman family. Let us hope we will survive this hell."

Isaac stayed until evening. We had dinner, and afterward I gave him food to take back. I gave money and thanks to his escort from the Jewish police.

Temporarily I was happy.

Chapter Eleven

The Ghetto Reduced

Less than a week later we were ordered to move back to the ghetto. No one was to sleep at the factory. Given only a few hours advance notice, we gathered together our belongings. The Jewish police arrived with horses and wagons to take us back to the ghetto.

Two nieces of one of the more wealthy men at Kromoloswky, Szyja Najman, asked me to help them hide in the factory, too terrified to return to the ghetto. I found a comfortable hiding place and told them to bring enough food for a few days when they went into hiding. I thought of my sister. I was grateful for the opportunity to help someone, as I would want her to be helped.

I was not prepared for the move, having given Isaac much money. Back in the ghetto with my 3,000 *zloty*, I paid to get a small room, a bed, and a few other things. Afterward I had only 250 *zloty*, yet despite my lack of money, I decided I would not risk my life anymore by doing business with the Polish at Kromolowsky. Now we had to walk to work every morning, escorted by a Jewish policeman under the supervision of an SS man. This did not last for long. After three weeks the SS liquidated this place of work.

The boundaries of the ghetto had been drawn tight, from Zytnia Street to Szwarlikowska, and from Rynek Street to Stare Miasto. Concentrated in this small neighborhood packed like sardines, we were easier for the Germans to control. The Ukrainians, a group of about eighty led by a born killer by the name of Kapke, assisted the Germans in killing our people. It was terrifying for us to see what was going on in the ghetto.

Approximately 3,000 of us remained after the liquidation of the Walowa Street ghetto. We were all that was left of a culture that had existed for hundreds of years.

Each day before work everyone was forced to assemble for the *Appel* (the counting) on Szwarlikowska Street at the ghetto gate. Under the supervision of the Jewish police, workers separated into groups by factory. Close to the gate, in front of everyone, the *Lagerelder* (supervisor) stood until the SS came into the ghetto with the *Lagerführer* (German official). A whistle blew and we moved through the gate in tight groups of 100, divided into twenty rows, each with one *Kapo* in front. The SS counted as we passed, writing the tally down in a book. On our walk to work in this formation, one of the SS led and the Jewish police followed.

Each morning after our departure from the ghetto, the Jewish police and the Ukrainians searched our houses to find any individual who remained behind without an *Arbeitscheine*. Many of us worked at night and slept during the day, but remained safe as long as we had an *Arbeitscheine*. The others were taken away, or killed by the Ukrainians on the spot. When not with the Jewish police, the Ukrainians demanded money and jewelry to spare people's lives. They also carried out searches for young children, who often hid in cellars. Some were killed on the spot, others were chased out into the streets toward the ghetto gate where they were collected and later taken away. These children never returned. At times their clothes were brought back, covered with blood, to be washed by women in the ghetto and sent to Germany to be worn by German children.

One of the jobs of the Jewish police was collecting on the sidewalks those who died of hunger and illness during the night. Each morning more than twenty bodies of our children lay on the sidewalks. They had crawled from their hiding places during the night to look for food. Too weak to survive, many died, still clutching bits of food. Their bodies were taken away in two-wheeled carts to Pentz Garden where they were buried.

The SS frequently came to the ghetto hospital, at times taking away the sick to be killed. If discovered, pregnant women were killed. In order to save the lives of women, the hospital director, Dr. Szenderowicz, performed abortions in secret, usually at night. Sometimes, the SS gave the sick to the Ukrainians who would kill them. This was their job—to kill.

Chapter Twelve

Winter 1942–43

The rain came and it seemed to have no end. Many with no wood or coal for heat and without warm clothing died from the cold. The wet clothes had to dry on our bodies. Shaking from the cold, we had to go on living with the hope of a better tomorrow, which never seemed to come.

Then the snow came. In the mornings as we ran out for our cup of coffee and piece of bread, our good fortune was not to be caught and made to shovel snow by the Jewish police. The police, knowing where the poor lived, sometimes came to make them clear the walkways for the SS to start their daily routine.

With Isaac still living at the *Waffen* factory, I lived alone in a little room on Szpitalna Street. It was terrible at night with no one to talk to and only one blanket to keep warm. I stared at the ceiling, shaking from coldness, thinking of the terrible things that happened a few months before, and crying. When eventually I did sleep, it was only for a short time, until the neighbors' knock awakened me for work.

With money I made at Kromolowsky, I paid the Jewish police to get a job as one of 800 turf cutters, gutting two-foot deep marshlands and carving peat blocks to be stacked by a female assistant. Though it was physically strenuous activity, with a quota of 800 blocks to be reached by four o'clock, I could do as I pleased once my quota was reached.

The 800 of us, overseen by a member of the SS, worked

in eight groups of 100 each, with one Jewish policeman supervising each group. The *Kapo* of my group, Usher Goldberg, was a friend with whom I had gone to *cheder* and gymnasium, and was a good person. My family had lived with him and his wife, Rywcia, at the estate of her parents, the Eismans, before moving to the ghetto.

Overall, circumstances were similar to those at Kromolowsky We pooled our money to pay the German supervisor, Buchmeyer, giving him gifts to overlook business we conducted with the Polish. Those of us too sick or old to reach the quota paid for the help of others.

As my money from Kromolowsky was nearly gone, I had to find a new source of income in order to buy warm clothes and food. The food ration, given my strenuous physical labor, was insufficient to keep me alive. I often went to bed hungry, with only a cup of coffee and piece of bread for breakfast, a bowl of watery soup and piece of bread for lunch, another bowl of soup and piece of bread for dinner.

My sole friends in the ghetto were two brothers, Fishel and Sam Borenkraut. Fishel, a friend of Isaac's, and his brother Sam would one day become my brothers-in-law when I married their sister Helen. Visiting their house after work, at times until very late, I sat close to the coal stove, resting before going tack to my cold room. It was at their house I met Sylverstrum, a baker to whom I soon made a business proposition, suggesting I sell his pastries on commission.

After quite a while Sylverstrum agreed to my plan. He began baking rolls at night, and I picked them up in the morning, placing up to fifty in two pouches sewn into my coat back. The possession of food or cigarettes presented a problem upon returning to the ghetto when searches were conducted by the

Jewish police. Walking to work, I went row to row selling the rolls, knowing Usher would keep an eye on the SS member at the front. By the time we arrived at our workplace, I had sold all the rolls. Only one little boy, Lutek, the younger brother of Moniek Den, a school friend of mine, did not pay, claiming each night to his parents that he had not taken a roll from me. I did not argue. I did not have time. I had to run to the houses and collect the money from the people who took the rolls from me. Then I would go to the baker and pay him and he would prepare rolls for me for the next morning.

One night after I had worked particularly hard all day, I picked up a special order of rolls from Sylverstrum, returned home, and collapsed on my bed in exhaustion, forgetting to close the front door. I was awakened by Lodia Tatarka and her brother, who stood by the door devouring the rolls. As I began to yell, they ran from the room, but most of the order was gone already. Not knowing how I would pay Sylverstrum, tears came to my eyes. Then I went downstairs to Rachmil Borenstein, one of the *Kapos* in the ghetto who was helpful, and never violent. After I explained my predicament, he went with me to Lodia's house to ask for payment.

Lodia said she and her brother had seen the rolls on my table and were so hungry they could not help themselves, but she had no money. Rachmil then took me to the baker and explained the situation to him. Sylverstrum asked me to please be careful as he had to pay for the ingredients himself. Feeling miserable, I promised to be careful. At least I had not lost my source of income. I was making so little, but it helped me to buy some extra food.

I still feel the moral torment of those moments.

Chapter Thirteen

"Exchange" of Intellectuals

One evening after work when I was not particularly tired, shortly before Purim of 1943, I decided to use the few hours before the 7:30 curfew to sell rolls to wealthy residents of the ghetto. Within two hours Sylverstrum had prepared an order for me, which I then took from house to house as quickly as possible. In the rush I knocked on a door I had not intended to.

The door opened and I went inside. As I offered the rolls for sale, I raised my eyes and saw several old friends playing cards and drinking wine. I felt humiliated, ashamed. I was dressed in shabby clothes, clutching a bucket of rolls, pleading for someone to buy from me so I could survive. I felt like a beggar. Quickly I backed out of the room and ran down the front steps. On the bottom step I sat down and cried. I prayed for strength to get through it all, and a voice somewhere inside me said this was not the end of the world, that I had to be strong in order to survive, that I would survive. I sat for a while, then got up and continued going house to house.

As I was selling my pastries I heard that the next morning the Germans planned to make an exchange of intellectual Jews for German prisoners. Dr. Szenderowicz had prepared a list of those in our ghetto who were to go. Many thought this was the last chance to get out of the hell we were in. The ones on the list were in good spirits, had their best clothes ready for the trip, and paid me extra, saying they no longer had to worry about money. Among those I spoke with were Dr. Banker Den, Dr. Tovia Korman, Jacob Kagan, Rabbi Zlotnick, and his wife and daughters.

I went to the Borenkrauts to discuss the turn of events. Sam was adamant that I should not go, convinced the Germans were using the idea of an exchange as a lure to the intellectuals who remained after the ghetto's liquidation. I went back to my room and mulled the matter over for a long time, alternately disturbed at the thought that all these people could be so naive, and happy at the thought that there was a way out of this hellhole.

In my reverie I fell asleep. The departure of those on the list awoke me. Going outside, I stood and watched as good-byes were said. Many of those remaining requested their letters and greetings be passed on to loved ones in Palestine. Maybe they are going to Palestine, I thought.

At exactly 8:30 A.M., the gate of the ghetto opened and there stood a group of armed Ukrainians, Kapke in their midst. A large truck backed toward the gate. The Ukrainians helped the people get into the truck. When it was fully loaded, they pulled down the cover, jumped in fast, and drove away. The SS stood in the distance and only watched. It happened very quickly. At that moment I thought, "The Germans are leaving the job for the Ukrainians to take care of our people who are going away to Palestine. They are the killers. There is something terribly wrong." My guardian angel said to me, "Joe, move away" Yes, he was watching over me. Slowly I backed away from the gate. Another truck backed up to the gate. It happened very fast. The same procedure. When full, the Ukrainians with machine guns over their arms pulled down the cover, jumped into the back of the truck and drove away. From the side street, a little truck drove to the front of the gate. Kapke, with the rest of the Ukrainians, jumped in and they drove away.

As I left, despite feeling disturbed by what I had seen, I still felt I might be missing my chance for freedom. Back in my room I slept for a while. The sound of crying from the streets woke me. Going outside I saw the Zlotnick sisters and Tovia and his sister, Bela Friedman, all of whom had left that morning by truck. Shaking, they said the Ukrainians had taken the road to Szydlowiecz and there they brutally murdered all but a few who had somehow convinced Kapke to spare their lives.

I remember the happy Purim which turned into a tragedy. A group of educated people, the few of so many thousands who had been saved at the time of the liquidation of the Jewish community in 1942 in Radom, had joined the millions of our people who had been killed as *Kiddish Ha-Shem* (martyrs).

Chapter Fourteen

Letters

I received a letter from my brother. Still at the *Waffen* factory, saying that he had fallen into very poor health from being overworked by the new foreman there. Holding the letter in my hands, I came to the conclusion that I had to get the money our father had hidden.

Fischel Borenkraut, at the time, worked in a military installation outside the ghetto. I asked for his help. After a short while he arranged for a German soldier to accompany us to where my father's boxes were hidden. Finding 100 British pounds, I paid the soldier and exchanged the rest in the ghetto for *zloty*, sending some to Isaac. Through a Jewish policeman I heard from Isaac that he was thus able to get work at the hospital at the Szkolna *Arbeitslager* (labor camp) and take care of his health.

With the remaining money, I began buying food from Poles who came to the ghetto gate at night. After they had run off with my money a couple of times, I made certain I had the food first. No more selling rolls. It was easier to buy food at the fence and sell it in the ghetto.

As my earnings increased from selling food, I bought some nice clothes, warm bedding, and sent Isaac money at the Szkolna Arbeitslager. Soon the Poles I did business with wanted only gold or jewelry, not money any longer. I had my wealthy customers pay in this manner, so I might continue to buy food. Living in the ghetto you never knew what surprises tomorrow would bring.

Helen Borenkraut, sister of Fishel and Sam, was one of a group of young women taken out of the ghetto prior to the liquidation in August of 1942. She had not been heard from since, until one morning Fishel received a letter from her saying she was in the Wolanow *Arbeitslager*, that she had contracted typhus, and did not know if she would survive.

Taking an enormous risk, Fishel paid a German soldier he worked with to drive him to the Wolanow *Arbeitslager* in an army truck. At Wolanow's gate, he paid one of the policemen to let them enter during the changing of the guard, found Helen, and took her back to the Walowa Street ghetto.

As Fishel knew the ghetto leader, he was allowed to take his sister to the ghetto hospital for treatment. But it was not long before someone denounced them to the Germans. The Jewish police arrived at the hospital with orders and took Helen, as well as Fishel, to the police station. The *Sturmbahnführer* in charge of the ghetto, Bloom, might have ordered their death but instead had Helen returned to the ghetto hospital and had Fishel released, but prohibited him from returning to work. It was the day of *Sturmbahnführer* Bloom's daughter's wedding, and he must have felt generous.

Dr. Szenderowicz, the ghetto elder, knew the Borenkraut brothers personally, and was therefore able to attend to Helen. When she was strong enough to leave the hospital, Fishel took care of her, asking me to buy cheeses, butter, cream, and milk. At work, still supervised by Buchmayer, whom we kept content with money and gifts, I was able to buy food from Poles who came to the workplace. I made a contraption of string to hold it inside my clothing in order to smuggle the food back into the ghetto. Helen fully recovered after two weeks.

Chapter Fifteen

Szkolna

The SS often took from the ghetto young, strong men to go to work. One day they chose thirty men, among them Szyja Najman's three sons. Mr. Najman kissed his sons good-bye, blessed them, and gave the SS quite a bit of money to take care of them. The SS promised to do so, as usual, with reassurances that there was no reason to worry. His sons were put to work under the *Sonderkommandos*, removing signs of SS atrocities as Germany retreated from Russian territory.

One day the SS was searching for workers. I hid with Fishel and Helen, which gave me the opportunity to talk with her. She was very bright and intelligent. I fell in love. A voice inside me said, "This is your girl."

The SS soon closed the ghetto completely and moved us to the Szkolna *Arbeitslager*, where my brother was. Isaac worked as a dental technician in the hospital, alongside Dr. Celniker; I received a job as an electrician at the *Waffen* factory. At first things went well. The SS paid for dental work with vodka, which I sold or exchanged for food at the factory. At times, after work, I sold the vodka in the barracks where we slept.

Occasionally I cooked a meal on the small stove at work, smuggling the food back to the barracks. I invited Helen and Fishel to Isaac's for dinner one evening, having prepared blintzes and soup. At some point I told my brother and Fishel of my feelings for Helen. Isaac responded, "Let's hope we survive this hell. Afterwards you can marry her." Fishel added, "Give her time. She is very young. If we survive, then you can tell her how you feel. It will be up to her."

The men's and women's barracks were divided, each fenced with barbed wire and under the watch of Ukrainian guards. I used to stay for hours looking through the wires. Tears came to my eyes feeling how terrible it was to love someone I could not be with, with no possibility of sharing the happiness of being in love. But thinking of Helen gave me the will to go on. I gave the Ukrainians vodka in order to be allowed into the women's barracks to see Helen in the evenings. My visits with her were among those unusual moments of happiness occurring under horrendous circumstances.

Not long after our move to Szkolna, there was a selection. My brother was chosen to go to the death camp Majdanek. The night before he was scheduled to leave, I tried unsuccessfully to persuade him to hide or accompany me to the factory for the day and return to the camp at night. I also pleaded with our *Lagerelder*, Chile Friedman, not to separate us, explaining we were the only two survivors of our family. Apparently, though I did not know it at the time of this conversation, Friedman had come to my father to buy leather at the beginning of the war, and my father refused him. His response to me was, "If you do not leave right in the next minute, I will send both of you to Majdanek."

My tears were unstoppable as I left. I was losing my brother. Sitting with him until late at night, I again tried to convince Isaac to go to the factory in the morning, but he was afraid to do so. His last words were, "Joseph, I am going. You stay here. Separated in two different places, there may be more chance one of us will survive." I felt the opposite was true.

As I kissed him good-bye, embarrassing him, I felt it would be the last time I ever saw him. Going back to my place, then lying in bed with my eyes wide open, I tried to think of what else I could do to help Isaac. It was terrible to helplessly watch him go to his death. He and I were the last of two hundred family members in the city of Radom.

When Isaac was taken to Majdanek, I lost the will to live. I lost contact with the Borenkrauts. I was alone and had no one to talk to once again, returning each day from work, lying in bed, reliving the horrible moments in which I lost my mother, my father, Tania, Elek, and Isaac.

Those of us who survived the Nazi slaughter lived in shock, having become almost inhuman. We no longer knew what to feel, how to behave. Many who lost the will to live died in this sleep.

The SS turned me into a robot; never thinking. I worked, ate, and slept, driven by fear of death. Somehow I retained a spark of hope.

Chapter Sixteen

Auschwitz

In July 1944, the SS liquidated the Szkolna *Arbeitslager* and we were all sent from the camp on a death march to Auschwitz. The march lasted a week or maybe a few days more as we walked at night, for the most part, and slept during the day in fields, all the while having no idea of our destination. The Russian army rapidly advanced behind us.

The weather was quite hot and there was little food or water. Many people died of thirst and exhaustion, and many others were killed by the SS, in particular the sick and old. Many were left dead on the road, and the SS did not take time to bury them, but hurried us onward. The children, once saved in the ghetto by their parents who gave money to the SS, now went with us to Auschwitz for use in experimentation, torture, and eventually death.

Very few of us tried to escape. We knew that some Poles turned Jews in for a mere pound of butter or sugar. Only the two Cynas brothers escaped. Luckily they survived by living in the forest. More than a week of marching ended with our arrival at Tomashow, where we were put in a warehouse a few days and then put onto cattle trains. In each train there were Germans, graduates of a special training school, the curriculum of which was methods of torture and killing. These specialists had learned to evoke in victims until the last moment of their lives the belief they could survive. It was easy to make us believe, easy to play on emotions of helpless people.

The train stopped at Auschwitz. Peering out of a barbwire opening in the cattle car, I saw an idyllic, lush garden of flowers and grass, and heard beautiful orchestral music. I saw people dressed in striped uniforms, and policemen with armbands, moving as though they were machines.

Quickly the women, the sick, and the old were pushed out of our trains. As they were taken, I peered out of the opening and saw a ramp with a group of SS before it. A handsome man stood at the group's front, dressed in a gray leather coat, a little stick in his hand. The police pushed the women toward the ramp and down it, all the while telling them to move more quickly.

This was the selection, though we did not know it, and the man in front was the infamous Dr. Mengele, the Angel of Death. Moving his stick to the left and to the right, he sent our loved ones to death or to torture followed by death. Our mothers. Our fathers. Our sisters. Little children, some holding their mothers' hands. A man named Mr. Frenkiel carried a little girl in his arms. I believe she was Glika Goldkorn's daughter. It was a parade of human material for the ovens of the extermination factory in Auschwitz.

The sounds of the loud voices of the SS, children crying, the pleas for help still ring in my ears. The police and the SS forced everyone into a run. As the police pushed them from both sides, the Germans, with dogs, chased those who could not move quickly.

Amid this horror an orchestra, situated across from the train tracks, played beautiful music. Nazi authorities gave special privileges to Jewish professional musicians who performed in the ensemble. The mellow strands from the musicians mixed with the horrifying sound of children crying created a surreal, chilling atmosphere. Mengele, waving his stick, seemed like a conductor, playing Master of Destiny. This terrible picture will stay with me as long as I go on living.

I wept as I watched, and smoke from the crematorium chimney made me choke. The smell of burning flesh reached us already, and we had not even stepped down from the train.

Chapter Seventeen

Vaihingen

After a few hours of waiting on the train, I was sent from Auschwitz to Vienna, kept briefly at Bahnof, then sent to the Vaihingen *Arbeitslager* for the next few weeks. There, though the conditions were worse than at Szkolna, it was still possible to survive. The people there were from Radom. Knowing one another made it easier.

We were to build an armament plant. Though the work was more strenuous, the routine was the same: morning *Appel*; quick breakfast of one cup of coffee and a piece of bread; work; lunch of another cup of coffee and a piece of bread; work; and in the evening after work, a cup of soup and a piece of bread.

The supervisor of the barrack was Elder Batler, a man who worked me excessively as he did not like me. After just a short while I became extremely ill and was hospitalized, unable to eat, running a fever, experiencing horrible pain in my stomach which had bloated up like a balloon, and every few minutes needing to run to the toilet, which was quite far, with diarrhea.

I no longer felt at all human. As I lay in bed I waited for the end.

Gimpel Weintraub, the close friend with whom I worked in the St. Kazimierza Hospital and in the disinfection department in the ghetto, was hospital director at the time. He had changed. I do not know what makes people change, what makes them forget all human feelings, all sense of morality, but

Gimpel had. He came and stood at the foot of my bed each day, passing out the soup rations. My portion represented the only means I had for recovery as no medication was given to patients. Gimpel looked at me as if to let me know he was the master, that he could play with me and take advantage of my misery. Sometimes he gave me half a ration. I looked at him and I cried, more from emotional than physical pain. I would prefer to think that it might be that he did not recognize me.

After two weeks, which seemed like an eternity, I was selected to be one of five hundred people to go to Schoemberg, a destination primarily for the sick and the old. For me this was extremely fortunate. Continuing as I was, in a few days I would have been dead.

Thrown into the cattle train, suffering from a severe case of dysentery, I could not sleep or eat at the beginning of our journey to Schoemberg. I simply lay in the corner, not moving, for two days drinking my ration of a cup of water and collecting my piece of bread to exchange for more water. On the third day, my fever subsided and I began to feel better, to move around, to recognize people around me and to feel hunger again. A young man lying next to me, whom I heard praying in Hebrew, told me he had watched over me to see that no one stole my bread. I thanked him. As we talked we became friends on this trip to the death camp. His name was Lester, a rabbi from Lodz. He came to the little ghetto with a group of printers from Majdanek in 1943.

Four or five days passed. The train began to travel at a slower pace. We heard airplanes. Then the train stopped, but we were not taken off. Kept inside, we received our daily ration each morning from the *Kapo*. One afternoon the SS ordered us out. As we stood waiting in front of the trains, several cars were driven up, followed by trucks of SS men. With dogs, the SS jumped from the trucks, conducted a count, put us in groups of one hundred, one *Kapo* each, and surrounded us. As a whistle blew, we were marched down the road to the death camp Schoemberg. We were not told which road it was, but only that we must move quickly.

Chapter Eighteen

Schoemberg

As surely as God lives, who has denied me justice The Almighty, who has made me taste bitterness of soul, as long as I have life within me, the breath of God in my nostrils, my lips will not speak wickedness, and my tongue will utter no deceit.

JOB, CHAPTER 27, VERSES 2, 3, 4

It was the beginning of October, 1944. The weather was still nice. The trees lining the road on both sides were changing colors, their leaves scattered on the ground. Close to five o'clock we came to the outside of the camp. The sign on its gate read *ARBEITSLAGER* SCHOEMBERG. Surrounded by both an eighteen-foot fence and a water filled ditch which ran along the outside of the fence, the camp was still under construction. We stood for half an hour. Then a whistle blew and the *Lagerelder* assembled the *Kapos* from each group. This *Lagerelder*, in charge of the *Kapos* reporting numbers coming in and out, was the first German I had seen in a striped uniform. After briefly speaking to the *Kapos*, he turned to us and announced we were to stay together and enter the camp when the

1. Political camps were different from death camps in that they held prisoners who were not deemed racially inferior but who had political disagreements with their Nazi captors. Such inmates wore red squares on their prison uniforms, insignias to distinguish them from other prisoners.

whistle blew. No talking was permitted.

The whistle blew. We passed through the gate. The main road was muddy and in terrible condition. As we walked toward the twenty-five barracks and horse stables, we tramped through mud eight to ten inches thick. At one point I lost my shoes and it took me quite a while to find them. We entered Barracks 3. The floor was covered with water, the roof half open, the frames of windows empty of glass, and one lamp stood in the middle of the room, giving little light. Pitka, a Russian *Kapo* in his early twenties, entered the barracks carrying a stick, his face clean shaven, his body enormously strong, attired in a Russian-style dark shirt, quilted pants, a hat, and black boots. He informed us that the barracks were under his authority and we must obey him. The Kapo who had come with us from Vaihingen, Rachmil Borenstein, the same man who had spoken to Sylverstrum for me in the ghetto, was taken aside by Pitka. After a brief talk, Pitka left and Rachmil informed us that Schoemberg was a "political" camp with inmates from all over Europe, that Jews were kept separate from the others, and that conditions were terrible.[1]

Responsible for the maintenance of our own barracks, we set to cleaning up under the supervision of the *Kapo*, until the bell rang, signaling the evening meal and Pitka returned. He spoke with our *Kapo* and took two men out of the barracks. When they returned, the two carried buckets of small plates with spoons. Receiving a plate and spoon each, Pitka warned us that if we lost them, we would have no meals. Again he left with two men who returned carrying a kettle of hot, watery soup, and small pieces of bread. In order to receive our ration, we stood in line in front of the barracks, without talking, for one hour as the SS paced on all sides.

An SS man approached me and asked if I understood German. I said I did. He said he would like to speak with me. After I received my ration, I accompanied this man and was given an extra piece of bread for doing so. The SS knew I had come from Vaihingen, he said, and they knew wealthy Jews were in my group. In exchange for gold pieces or jewelry these people could receive extra bread or soup, he said, and if I facilitated this, he would take care of me and see that I was provided with plenty of food. I agreed to carry out the exchange. After asking my name, he showed me where he would wait for me the next evening when dinner was over.

I repeated the conversation to the rabbi I met on the journey to Schoemberg. Lester believed I would be killed if I did as the SS man asked.

Returning to the barracks, tired, still hungry, I took out a piece of bread I saved from the train and shared it with Lester. We ate, and then cleared a relatively dry space on the ground in order to sleep. Pitka returned and announced that in two to three weeks construction and furnishing of our barracks would be complete. There would be beds, and an oven for heat.

Chapter Nineteen

First Day

My job was to move stones. I moved them from one spot to the next from which they were moved by other workers. In this way a road leading to the camp was built.

On my first day of work, the SS asked men to do a job that would earn an extra piece of bread, so I volunteered. One hundred of us were taken to the railroad station where a shipment of building materials had come in. Unloading 150 sacks of cement, I carried some on my back up a hill of over a hundred feet. An SS member with a dog followed behind and forced me to move quickly. I finished and was ordered to take the sacks back down the hill. As I did so the SS supervisor chased me, with his dog barking, until I began to lose my breath and my legs ached. The dog got hold of me and bit me. I began to cry, but still was forced to carry the sacks. Dizzy, I fell. The dog ripped at my pants, and finally the SS pulled him off me. I stood up, still crying. The SS told me to finish the job. Crawling, I reached the hilltop and brought the remaining few sacks and collapsed. Blood came from my mouth. Tears came to my eyes and I passed out.

I regained consciousness to see the SS standing over me laughing. Handing me an apple and a piece of bread, he said I had done a good job, and left me to rest for a while. When he returned, I was taken back to my group, so exhausted I could not move. I stood and cried.

Back in the barracks that evening, I was approached by the Richtmans and the Kormans, two families from Radom who had been on the same train from Vaihingen to Schoemberg and had observed my conversation with the SS the evening before. They asked if I would get them food in exchange for money. Finding the SS wanted gold pieces and jewelry, they brought these and I promised to try to get them food. Meeting the SS as agreed, I gave him gold chains, diamonds, and a few pieces of gold. In exchange, he gave me a loaf of bread cut up into pieces and a pot of soup.

Upon returning to the barracks, I gave the *Kapo* a piece of bread, and the rest to the Richtmans and Kormans who, in turn, gave me a small piece for my services. I again went to meet with the SS, giving the bread to Lester for safekeeping. The apple and piece of bread I then received made me quite happy as I felt I had found a means to obtain extra food to share with Lester.

During the next two weeks I continued to do business with the SS. Then it came to an end.

Chapter Twenty

Order

Day after day we followed the same routine. We awoke to the sound of a whistle and the SS shouting *"Raus! Raus!"* ("Out! Out!"). Quickly we lined up outside the barracks in groups of one hundred, four to a row, in order of height, the tallest in front. The *Kapo* stood before us. The *Lagerführer*, record book in hand, passed as he conducted the count, including the dead, laid in rows of ten. Dead or alive, the numbers had to match those in his book. Finding those missing was the job of the *Kapo* and we all had to wait until everyone was accounted for. Anyone caught hiding received twenty lashes in front of the group, serving to warn the rest of us.

Every morning we stood in the cold for hours as the *Appel* was conducted. Hungry, half-naked, often without shoes, at times with rain frozen on our heads and mud frozen around our feet, many collapsed. Anyone who did so was subjected to a beating with wooden sticks, carried out by the *Kapo* and his assistants as the SS looked on, laughing and yelling, *"Macht schnell!"* ("Finish quickly!"). The beating continued until the body turned red, until there was little or no movement, no crying. Whoever was next in the row, on command, dragged the body to the pile of dead at the corner of the camp behind the fence to the toilet. Even if there was still some movement, some life, the body was left to be sprayed with chemicals by the Germans and, in the morning, buried in a ditch or burned in an open pit. After the *Appel*, the SS chose a few strong men from each group to dispose of the dead. Those who did the job received an extra piece of bread.

Signaling that the count for the day was correct, a whistle blew and we were forced to run like animals and line up for a cup of cold, very dark liquid which was supposed to be coffee, and a small piece of bread. Shaking from cold, aching from hunger, we hurried to get our rations as the *Kapos* stood over us, in front of us, to the side of us, ordering us to move more and more quickly. After the hour it took for all of us to get our rations, we ate quickly and assembled in front of the camp gate, where we stood in designated order, *Kapos* at the head, and were counted by the *Lagerelder*, then went out to work.

The *Kapos* in front, the SS with German shepherds on both sides, we marched in order for two hours to our place of work, a mile and a half away. Upon first arriving at the camp we had marched at a normal pace, but each day we moved a little slower. Many were sick and could barely walk, needing to be supported by others. Those who fell could not be helped up again. The oncoming rows stepped over the fallen, sometimes crushing them. Men in the last row of each group pulled the dead to the side of the road. Half-dead, screaming, people were left until the evening, collected then to be brought back with us to be counted. The SS chose strong men from last rows of the groups to drag the dead back. If there were hundreds, trucks were used. At the camp gate, our numbers had to match the morning count.

Once we passed through the gate, the bell rang for the evening meal. The same procedure was followed. An hour's wait until we all received our rations. Everyone had their own aluminum plate with a spoon attached to it by string. If the dish was lost, dinner was missed. Given the small size of our rations, a meal was a matter of life or death. A small pot of water, a piece of bread, these equaled a person's life. Survival was all the more difficult because the barracks had no heat for four weeks. Every night people died from cold. The sick that were sent to the hospital never returned.

Chapter Twenty-One

Lester

There was no water in the camp after weeks without washing, shaving, or changing our clothes, we smelled and looked nearly inhuman. At night insects attacked us, and the rain poured in from the still unfinished roof. We lay in water. Our clothes froze against our skin. Many died from the cold.

Throughout the night Pitka checked on us every few hours to make sure no one moved. Anyone who was out of place, he beat with a wooden stick. Afterward he called upon the *Kapo* to stand watch by the door in between his rounds. Though it was dangerous to move, I inched toward Lester, hoping to get some warmth. Afraid to fall asleep, he and I talked about one of the Hebrew poets, Bialik, and we competed to see which of us remembered more of his poetry. Lester had a wealth of knowledge.

Each morning when we were woken up, Lester took water from the ground, washed his face, and said the morning prayer quietly. Rushing into line for the *Appel*, he stood with eyes closed until he finished his prayer. With his unbroken will, this man was my inspiration. When I was insane from cold and misery, he said to me, "Hold on. As long as we are alive, we have hope. You will see someone in our group survive. There were times like these before in the history of our people and we endured. We have not been forgotten." A man of six feet, even with back bent over and face covered with dirt, his dark, and black eyes were full of life when he looked at someone, and his speech was powerful. When he spoke about God his eyes sparkled.

I told Lester about the loss of my family, and about Helen, whom I had not seen since Auschwitz. I had fallen in love with her. Often my thoughts of finding her and starting a new life gave me courage to continue to Schoemberg. When Lester heard me call her name and cry in my sleep, he spoke to me to give me courage.

On cattle trains, people were brought in every few days from all over Europe, from other camps, their arms marked with various symbols. List in hand; during the *Appel*, the SS took others away. New SS men arrived. The guards were changed. More brutal, they shoved us with their guns, yelling, "Stinking Jews." Feeling physically dead, as if I were a moving shadow, it was only spiritual strength that kept me alive.

One day during our fourth week, we were made to strip off our clothes and stand in line to be shaved. The *Kapo* doused the pile of our clothing with gasoline and set it on fire. I stood in line with Lester. Waiting in the cold, many collapsed. Those who did were beaten. The barbers, tall, strong Ukrainians and Russians, shaved our bodies from head to toe. Next came the "bath house." Each of us received a small piece of soap resembling glue, and stood on the concrete floor in the middle of the room under showers. We washed. My body had become very thin. The soap we were given was not easily dissolved. I still feel its texture now. This experience is very painful for me to relive; the memory of it still leaves me shaking.

Still wet, we were rushed to a barracks the sign on the front of which read *Bekleidugnsamt* (clothing department). The man in charge was a political prisoner, a German. We received striped jackets, short shirts, pants, and shoes. We dressed. As Lester's shoes were too small, he tried on mine. They fit him and we made an exchange. Hurrying to the evening meal, we were interrupted and hurried off again to new sleeping quarters by Pitka and his assistants. Our new barracks were two levels, with wooden bunkers lining the walls and a fireplace in the center. Lester and I were assigned beds on the lower level. Warm and clean, the new quarters made us feel somewhat better.

After only a few days, my leather shoes had rubbed my feet so raw they were bleeding and swollen. In order to make rags for my feet, I went to the place where the dead were collected one evening and took a pair of pants from one of the bodies. Back in the barracks, Lester and I ripped the pants and wrapped the rags around my feet. It was about this time that I began to try to find out how many people from Vaihingen were still alive. I could find only two. Not one of the Kormans was still alive. Only one son of the Richtmans family and Israel Isenberg were still around.

Soon another group was brought to our barracks, increasing the number of inmates to five hundred. The new group stayed together and did not speak. Their movements were very slow and quiet, their skin yellow, their bodies thin. When we had a chance to speak, we found they had been brought to Schoemberg from all over Europe. In broken German, crying, they told us their horror stories. Those who survived the trip to Schoemberg were here only so the SS could finish the job.

We were tired and hungry, but at least it was warm inside. Still, it was not easy to sleep after hearing such horrible stories from the people who had been assigned to our barracks. Lester said to me, "Human suffering has no end, but we are alive."

"Rabbi, why must we the chosen people suffer so much?" I asked. "Where is God? Why is God not helping us?"

"Joseph," he said, "remember I'm a servant of the Lord. I believe in the Almighty." Then Lester told me he witnessed the killing of his loved ones and lost his family but had not lost his faith in God. "I believe this is the darkest moment in the history of our people. It is a test and we must hold onto our belief."

"For how long must we go on suffering?" I asked.

His answer was that he did not know and he could not tell me. He stopped for a while, shaking his head and started his evening prayers. After he finished, he turned to me, "Joseph, believe. Believe in the Lord and the Lord will help us. Without belief it is not possible to hope."

This man gave me courage to believe in a tomorrow, which we did not have in this place of the dead.

The next morning Lester fell asleep in the line for food rations. As he stood there, his head bent forward and touched one of the passing SS. The man grabbed him, pushed him from the line, and hit him with a gun until Lester fell. Yelling, "Dirty Jew!" the SS jumped again and again on top of Lester's body. Lester's cries of desperation will never leave me. He called out in Yiddish for God to help him. The SS, angered by his cries, hit him until he fell silent. As the SS moved away, the Russian Kapo, Pitka, and his assistants hit Lester with wooden sticks until he was motionless.

Pitka ordered me to take Lester to where the dead bodies were collected. Helped by two other people, I carried Lester away. With what was left of life in him, Lester whispered, "Remember, Pitka is responsible for my death. If you survive, take revenge."

His dying words were, "*Shema Israel Adonai Elohenu Adonai Ehad.*" ("Hear, O Israel: The Lord is our God, the Lord is One.") To the last minute of his life, he did not lose his belief in the Almighty.

It has taken me years to write of these things. Words cannot convey what my experiences at this time were. As Lester died, I felt as if I too were dying.

We laid him gently on the mound of bodies and, as Pitka and his assistants stood behind us, I said the first verse of Kaddish. Forced quickly back in line, I stood there, crying and crying. I raised my eyes to the sky and asked quietly, "Lord, why did he have to be killed? He was your servant."

That night I cried for hours. Finally, when I fell asleep, I dreamed of Helen stretching her hand out to me. Someone in a bed near me began to worry I had died and gave me a push. I awoke. The night was very still. As the moon shone through the window, a feeling of how good it was to be alive returned to me.

I will treasure the memories of Lester all my life.

In the death camps God was dead. The Almighty is alive where humans live. Humanity stopped at the gate of the concentration camps. As for God, only the belief in Him existed. This was the only thing keeping us going, helping us to survive.

Chapter Twenty-Two

Lying with the Dead

The beginning of November. Standing for the *Appel* for over an hour, I was covered with a few inches of snow. My feet had begun to swell again. As I shook the ice from my head, it struck one of the passing SS. He turned around, grabbed me, and threw me to the ground and kicked me in the head. He then pulled out a knife and cut my head and back. I feel the pain now as I write about it. The scar on my back is twelve inches long.

It was so many years ago.

I screamed in pain. My blood spurted onto the SS man's uniform. Pitka gave him a towel. He tried to remove the blood and it was this that saved my life. One more cut with his knife and my head would have been severed. The SS moved away and Pitka and his assistants came, hit me with a crow bar, and kicked me until my cries were silenced. They then dragged me by the legs and threw me on the mound of dead bodies. Beneath me, some of the people were still alive. Blood flowed from their wounds. There was crying. After a few hours, the crying grew fainter.

Within a few hours a solution was sprayed over us. I passed out.

At night, maybe I was dreaming, but I thought I heard Helen call out my name. Half frozen, I reached out to where I heard the voice come from and fell from the mound. Again I passed out.

I woke up covered with blood and excrement. Without enough strength to lift myself, I crawled through the snow and mud for more than an hour. It seemed more like a hundred years, an eternity.

As I recall these moments now, I am trembling.

I crawled toward the hospital. Finally as I reached the door, someone opened it. My head struck the door. Looking up I saw a face from another world, a face I knew from when I studied in Warsaw. He had been a Polish medical student and I had seen him every Sunday at the symphony concert. I called out his name, "Wladek," and passed out.

When I awoke he was standing over me, crying. "Joseph, it's a miracle that in this death camp so far from home you recognized me." He told me that when I called out his name, he bent over me, pushed the blood and dirt from my face, and cried, "Don't worry," he said. "I will do whatever I can to save you." Despite the danger to himself, he treated my head and neck wounds. Again, I had found a friend.

As he gave me a cup of water, Wladek spoke to me, as though to a small child. "Now remember . . . I'll put you into the chamber where the dead are collected, but don't worry. . . I'll be back before the morning *Appel*. At that time only my assistants and I will be here. I will take care of you."

Laying me down in the chamber for the dead, he placed a few blankets over me, reassuring me it would be safe there. Between the rows of dead, I fell asleep. At 4:30 A.M. he returned. Removing the blankets from my legs, he told me not to move during the daily *Appel*, conducted by the *Lagerführer* between 6:30 and 7:00. The count was by legs; two legs, one number.

For over two weeks I remained in this chamber. There, the

dead lay in rows ten feet apart, at times more than forty in a row. Every morning before the *Appel*, Wladek removed the blanket from my legs and, as the *Lagerführer* walked between the rows, the touch of his stick reminded me I was alive.

Chapter Twenty-Three

Hospital in Schoemberg

I grew stronger. Wladek entered one morning with a white uniform in his hands. "Joseph, don't worry," he said. "You'll be my assistant." We left the mortuary and I felt like I was going from death to life. We went to the hospital.

The sign outside the hospital read *KRANKENHAUS*. Like the barracks, originally it had been a horse stable. A house of misery, it was little warmer than the barracks. Whitecoated men and the nurses wore striped uniforms underneath. Two hundred or so people lay on wooden beds, covered with blankets, their bodies immobile, their skin yellow, the odor from their open wounds terrible. They resembled skeletons more than the living. Some of them were lying quietly, just following us with their eyes as we passed by These had been *musselmen*, those who gave up all hope. Now they were living death, these last minutes before they died.

Each morning before the arrival of the *Lagerführer*, we carried the dead to the collection chamber, washed the faces of patients, straightened blankets, put beds against the wall, opened windows to air out the rooms, and cleaned the floor. Wladek stood at the front door at 7 A.M., with the list of the sick, the dead, and the hospital workers in hand. The *Lagerführer* approached, they exchanged salutes, and Wladek submitted the list to him. Going from bed to bed, then through the rows in the chamber for the dead, the *Lagerführer* counted each person with his bamboo stick. We followed ten feet behind, in accord with the rules. When the *Lagerführer* left, Wladek sighed with relief. One day he cried and told me that the day before his arrival at the hospital, the previous doctors had been killed for getting the numbers wrong. They had lost the paperwork of an order with which the SS took someone out of the hospital.

After the morning *Appel*, the nurses brought food from the kitchen and the patients were fed. Receiving our daily rations before the rest of the camp, we had plenty of food, enough so that I began to gain weight within a few weeks. After all, I thought, I might survive. Though it was not easy in the hospital, it was an improvement over the barracks. Each day I washed and hung to dry the bandages I made out of sheets, cleaned patients' wounds, and swept the rows between the dead. This was torture for me. At times, I said Kaddish for my friends who were among the dead and I cried. I had to move quickly to clean this place for the inspection. This was my daily job.

The operating room, kept very clean, held a large wooden table with three belts, and two small tables, one with scalpels, scissors, knives, and a hacksaw, the other with steel bars. To the side stood a fireplace. As assistant I stood by Wladek while he performed amputations, often with one cut. Open wounds he cauterized with steel bars heated in the fireplace. I held cloth in the patients' mouths, as there was no anesthesia, no medication. When patients cried out, an SS man came in and struck them. We could not interfere. Occasionally I helped Wladek with the operations. The crying, the smell of burning flesh was horrible.

New patients were brought into the hospital every evening. Wladek saved many, but only temporarily. All eventually died.

It was a mortuary, not a hospital.

Sleeping in the same room, Wladek and I at times talked until late. We talked of when we knew each other in Warsaw and he related to me stories of the uprising of Poles in Warsaw against the Germans in 1944. He was captured by the SS and was spared only because he was a doctor, wearing a red cross armband. Hundreds of thousands were killed by the Germans. The Russian army, not far from Warsaw, did nothing, allowing the Germans to do the dirty work of eliminating the opposition, eliminating the Polish patriots who dreamed of a democratic Poland. The Polish democrats fought alone, knowing they would die, and dying with honor. As I saw Wladek cry, I wondered how many of his friends had been killed. Afterwards, he was briefly at another hospital in territory the Germans were forced to retreat from, and then brought to work at Schoemberg. I told him about the selections in Auschwitz, and how Helen and the other women had remained behind and I was sent to Germany.

Some nights the SS came in, handed us an order, and took someone from the hospital, never bringing him back. Keeping these orders for the *Lagerführer* was a matter of life and death for us. The count had to be verified the next morning. It was my responsibility to keep the receipts and to count the sick and the dead. Those taken from the hospital, we soon found out, were people reported for hiding gold and jewelry. Their valuables confiscated, they were killed.

One day I left routinely to obtain the list of the sick returning from work. When I got back, Wladek was nowhere in sight, despite strict orders to be on the premises at all times. Suddenly the sharp stick of the *Lagerführer* touched my back and I thought it was the end. "Joseph, you are now responsible for the hospital," he shouted. "If it is not in order, you will pay with your head."

He left and I went into shock. In charge of the hospital. In charge of a house of misery and death. It was later, in the evening, that kitchen workers told me the SS had taken Wladek, this man of exceptional character, outside and drowned him in a ditch of water along with one other person. Afterwards they buried both victims.

I lost another friend. Again I was alone, nobody to talk with.

Using what Wladek had taught me, I tried to help the sick, at times forced to perform operations on half-dead bodies. People around me were dying. I tried to help them. How can you help a wounded man without medication? I cried saying the last prayers. They died in my arms.

Suddenly typhus broke out. The SS brought antibiotics to the hospital. As I gave injections, they stood at my back, shouting at me to move faster. In one hour I gave 300 shots, forced to repeatedly use the same needles. When my hand would no longer move, I turned to one of the SS and said he could kill me. I could not move. Hitting me with his gun, he pushed me away. One of the nurses was ordered to take over.

The patients were already dying from typhus. The injections were useless.

Chapter Twenty-Four

Transports

In December 1944, two weeks after Wladek was killed, I was roused by the shouts of an SS man as he pounded on my door. Quickly putting on my uniform, I was ordered to follow him to the camp gate. There the *Lagerführer* waited with a group of SS men whose machine guns were trained on a line of twenty-five trucks. The trucks pulled into camp and out climbed men in striped uniforms, so thin they looked like skeletons. Lined up by the sides of the trucks, they were counted, then the sick and wounded were divided from the strong.

As SS men indicated, I was to take charge of the sick, letting me know not by words, but by pointing at them. Already I knew the orders regarding this group. They were to be put in a hospital room apart from other patients, and to be "readied for slaughter." As the SS took the strong to a special barracks, with the help of a few of the nurses, I gathered the two hundred and fifty or so sick and took them to the hospital. They moved silently. Most of them, barely able to move, supported each other as they walked. Their legs were cuffed and half-frozen, their feet were bare. One young man, speaking in broken German, told me that three weeks earlier they had been suddenly taken out of a death camp in trucks as the Russian army drew near. The Russian air force bombarded the trucks along the road, forcing them to travel only at night. Of the sixty trucks they started out with, most were lost. Many prisoners were killed by the SS or died from cold and hunger, having received only one cup of warm water and one piece of bread a day. The weaker were left on the road.

Those of us working at the hospital did what we could to care for the new arrivals, bathing them and providing as much clothing as we could. It was five o'clock in the morning before we finished. I took a short nap.

The morning *Appel*. I knew what was required on that day before the *Appel*.

An SS man arrived with an order for fifty individuals from among the new arrivals to be taken from the hospital and be killed. He handed me the order, and had me accompany him to Barracks 2 of the hospital. Entering, he passed by the beds of the still sleeping, and moving quickly, he selected the fifty. Weak as these people were, it took two nurses fifteen minutes to move them out of the barracks and into the waiting truck.

Quickly I checked on the number of patients in preparation for the arrival of the *Lagerführer*. At 7:00 he conducted the *Appel*. Upon completion, he nodded his head. My numbers were correct. I had another day to live.

After two weeks I became very ill, both physically and emotionally, unable to eat or sleep, tortured by visions of severed body parts whenever I closed my eyes. Fortunately for me, among those who arrived in one of the new transports was a Russian doctor who was able to improve my conditions somewhat.

One day, while I was still ill, a *Kapo* told me of a transport leaving the next morning for the death camp Spaichingan, where it was rumored that conditions were better. For a cup of soup and a piece of bread he arranged for me to leave with the transport. The next morning, the *Kapo* arrived at the hospital. I quickly went into the chamber for the dead, changed my clothing, discarded my white uniform, and went with him.

Put onto two trucks, given half a loaf of bread each, one hundred of us were sent to Spaichingen.

Chapter Twenty-Five

Spaichingen

All my intimate friends detest me; those I love have turned against me. I am nothing but skin and bones; I have escaped by only the skin of my teeth.

JOB, CHAPTER 19, VERSES 19-20

As we traveled, the SS stopped once to conduct a count and to ensure that the backs of the trucks were securely shut. A few hours later, they again stopped. This time they shouted, "*Raus!*" Assembled in front of the trucks, one SS in front of each group, we were again counted, then given a cup of water and piece of bread. Ordered back into the trucks, we continued on the journey for the rest of the night, approximately eight more hours.

Upon arrival at Spaichingen, a small town near Stuttgart, the SS rushed from the trucks. We stood in groups in front of the vehicles, one *Kapo* at the head of each group. The *Sturmbahnführer* in charge of Spaichingen approached with a new group of SS, received papers from the SS accompanying us, conducted a count, and signed the papers. A whistle blew and we were directed toward the camp gate, the sign on which read, *ARBEIT MACHT FRET* (Work Makes One Free). A brick wall approximately eight feet high topped by barbwire surrounded the camp and was guarded by an SS man with dogs. Smaller then Schoemberg, the camp had only nine barracks housing approximately two hundred and fifty inmates each.

February 20, 1945 was the day we entered this new place of misery. Immediately we were sent to be shaved, to shower, and to receive new striped uniforms of shirts, pants, coats, and caps. In addition, we received new shoes and, quite unusually, underpants and undershirts. Assigned to Barracks 3, upon entering I was surprised to discover a friend of mine, Chaim Schluftman, with whom I had attended gymnasium. He and I subsequently spent many nights talking, sharing stories. In our talks, I told him of leaving Schoemberg without papers, and of my fear I would be caught and killed for this.

Despite my fears, I had an easier time at Spaichingen. The barracks were warm, clean, and furnished with wooden beds and blankets. The dishes consisted of metal plates with forks and spoons, and meals were given three times a day. Breakfast consisted of a cup of dark water (again, alleged to be coffee), and a piece of bread. Lunch and dinner both consisting of a watery, warm soup and piece of bread.

The work the SS had us do at this time was of a different nature. Each day, in nearby cities, we cleaned streets and removed rubbish from houses destroyed by bombers. We soon learned that the bombers had been American ones. Crying over the destruction of their homes, these were the first Germans I had seen shed tears. Though I felt sorry civilians were suffering, I was glad to have survived long enough to see Germans pay a price for the war they started, to see their dreams were shattered, too.

It was also at this time that I first received help from a German. A traffic policeman, over sixty years old and very heavy, who had been assigned to watch over our work called me to the side and gave me a small package of food on the second day.

Gesturing for me to eat, he stood and watched until I finished, afterwards taking me back to the group.

After a short while we began the additional work of constructing temporary housing for Germans in the form of barracks outside the cities. On March 10, 1945, the SS closed Spaichingen completely. Confined inside, we waited in dread. Shortly thereafter, fifteen hundred of us were marched southward to Bavaria via snowcovered side roads. With planes flying overhead, we walked at night and slept by day under trees. Given only a cup of water and a piece of bread a day, people grew sick and died, while the SS remained well fed with the supplies brought along by truck.

After two weeks, barely able to walk, moving like shadows, we were joined by a group recently marched out of another camp by the SS. Among them I discovered a man I knew from Radom, Leo Goldfarb, who had been in the tannery business and quite wealthy. His face nearly inhuman, his body deteriorated, his ankles swollen, he could no longer even speak, but only make noises. Tears came to his eyes when I called his name and he saw me. The next morning an SS man ordered two people to drag him into the bushes. The two returned and shortly we heard shots. When the SS returned I asked what happened to my friend, and he said, "I killed him."

As we continued down the road, Chaim Schluftman and I walked beside each other. He cried over Goldfarb's death and said Kaddish. I felt so miserable, so sick, and constantly hungry, so much so that I could barely understand or remember what was going on around me. My body was skin and bones. Desperate for nourishment, I added grass to my water.

On April 26 I collapsed on the road to Munich. Sick to my stomach, aching, crying, I passed out.

PART THREE

Rebirth

The Lord blessed the latter part of Job's life more than the first. And he also had seven sons and three daughters. After this Job lived a hundred and forty years; he saw his children and their children to the fourth generation.

JOB, CHAPTER 42, VERSES 12, 13, 16

Chapter Twenty-Six

Liberation

At 4:30 a.m. on April 26, 1945, I found myself lying on the side of the road thirty-six kilometers from Munich, only half alive, shaking from the cold. Thundering and streaks of light came from the distance. Afraid to move, I just lay with my eyes wide open looking around. I felt pain in my stomach from hunger. Near me columns of people passed without a sound: death camp evacuees, civilians pushing small carts, and German soldiers, wounded and unarmed.

As the sun approached the horizon, the thunder grew increasingly louder. People increased their pace, pushing one another, running along the side of the road. Army trucks, followed by soldiers on foot, rolled down the middle. I later found out they were General Patton's Third Panzer Division, which had broken through German lines.

With my last bit of strength, I tried to rise, but again passed out, for how long I do not know. Upon opening my eyes I found an American soldier over me. His face was sweaty, his eyes filled with tears. He had been trying to rouse me by poking me with his gun. I made a noise and he laughed. Tears ran down his cheeks. His words as he called out to the other soldiers still ring in my ears. "Hey, fellows, here is one more still alive." Wiping the filth from my face, he poured water over my forehead. A small amount he poured into my mouth. I began to cry, this time with tears of joy. I had been through so much pain I could no longer remember how to smile.

With another soldier, he very gently lifted me into a jeep. They spoke to me comfortingly, quietly, and gave me a piece of chocolate and a few crackers. Having not seen chocolate for a very long time, I held it in my hand. The soldier gestured for me to eat. I cried. I could not eat. Shortly an American chaplain approached and spoke to me in German, telling me not to fear anymore: "You are free."

I hardly believed what I was hearing. The circumstances I had passed through and those I now found myself in were incomprehensible. I was free at last. I had survived and yet in the final hours before liberation so many of my friends had died.

Chapter Twenty-Seven

Hospital in Fussen

I was taken by the Americans to a hospital in Fussen where I was well cared for. Bathed, shaved, and helped into a new pair of pajamas, I was taken to bed by the nurses. I stood beside it, stunned, patting it with my hands. I had not seen a clean bed for many years. All I could think of was the hospital beds in Schoemberg. I sat on the floor and cried. Those around me cried as well.

After a few moments the nurses gently lifted me onto the bed. It was not easy for me, the shadow of death still before my eyes. It took me quite a while to lie down. Lying on the bed I was crying quietly. It was not so easy for me. I would close my eyes and the faces of my friends would appear in front of me. Exhausted, I finally fell asleep. Upon awakening, I again began to cry, very loudly. The nurses came in and quieted me. With the kindness of everyone in the hospital, I was nursed back to health.

During my first breakfast I put two pieces of bread under my pillow. For the next three weeks I put bread in the drawers. Then I began to understand that the deprivation was over, the morning beatings were over, and the severe pain was over. I was free. My fear of venturing outside the hospital, of being hurt by someone, began to subside and I wandered through Fussen, a beautiful city in the mountains. Yet each time I saw a German with gray hair I thought how he was among those who killed my loved ones; each time a German smiled at me I wondered how he could when just yesterday Germans killed millions of innocent people. Seeing such normal looking people on the streets, I asked myself what made them change, what made them kill millions, where their morals were and where was their voice of reason?

Many times I ran to get back to the hospital where I felt safe. The nights were very hard for me. Repeatedly I had nightmares of the slaughter, the mountains of bodies, the loss of my loved ones and my mother calling out to me as my sister held her and they were taken away. Lying sleepless many nights I asked myself what to do next, where to go, where I might start a new life. A man without a past, I found myself alone in a strange country, in a country whose people had done so much harm to my family, my people, and me. With no one to share the moment of freedom, I was left alone with my terrible memories, trying to justify why I had survived, trying to encourage myself to go on living.

One day, having walked to the marketplace at the center of the city, I stood admiring a sculpture of Poseidon, the Greek god of the sea, surrounded by children. Noticing children nearby laughing and playing, I realized I had not seen children play for six years. As I stared at them, memories flooded me of children thrown from second- and third-story windows, of children crushed beneath the boots of the SS.

In tears, I approached the children. Touching the chin of a little girl, I thought how she was no different from the innocent children murdered but for the fact she was born to German parents. This gave her the right to live. As I raised my eyes to the sky, I asked God why our children had to die. Suddenly a woman rushed from a house nearby and pulled the little girl away. I was left thinking of how this same woman who rushed to protect her child might yesterday have thrown our children into the ovens. Do Germans still have feelings of love? Are they still human? "Where is justice?" I cried bitterly, remembering the past.

Back at the hospital, having run the entire way, I lay on my bed, shaking, trying not to think. It was so hard to face reality. My wounds still fresh, I was having trouble stepping from death back into life. It is not so easy for me to recall the time after my liberation. I was still suffering.

Though my overall physical condition improved, the left side of my head became so swollen that I could not use my left eye. The pain was constant. Fearing German doctors would not care for me, to my good fortune I was sent to a nerve specialist. He was Swiss, a man in his seventies known for many years by the hospital director who was an American. After being under the specialist's care for three weeks, I was cured. During those weeks I spent many hours in his office relating my experiences of the last six years, happy to have someone to talk to. It had been so many years since I had not had pain. I could now see from my left eye.

I did not like living in Germany, seeing it only as a slaughterhouse, a cemetery, its soil soaked with blood. The country, Germany, was a constant reminder of my personal moral and physical suffering. It was only after a while that I made peace with being there.

I will never forget the generation of Germans from yesterday. They took things from me which are irreplaceable. They took my past, my beginning. I was a man without a past, a man who was afraid to look for the future. We humans have to have memories. We could not live without the past and this the Nazis tried to take away from us, our feeling of belonging. They did not succeed though. We kept on looking until we found ourselves. It was not easy after all we had been through to be normal again. Yes, we saw the angel of death. When a human sees death this is the end. We saw it. And yet we came back.

Yes, this is my second life.

I'm a child of the Holocaust. I was born into my second life at the moment when the Nazis killed my mother, the one who had given me life. They turned her into a handful of ashes. I became a wandering Jew, one thousand years old, without a home. When the American came to save me he gave me back my Jewish name, "Joseph," like Moses in Egypt who in his little cradle was floating on the Nile River, just as I was floating on a mountain of a million bodies of my people. Their innocent blood was like the Nile River. The song of my birth was the sound of our children being tortured and ripped into pieces while still alive. Their voices, full of pain, was my blessing, reminding me to go on living, never to forget their broken dreams. One and a half million children killed by the Nazis, the dreams of our children interrupted so tragically.

One day in the nearby town of Feldafing, I miraculously found an American-supervised displacement camp of thousands of survivors from the death camps. For the first time since the liberation, I saw people from Radom, including two brothers of a friend of mine named Baum, and four of Helen's brothers. Helen's brother, Fishel, my very good friend, was killed in Dachau a few hours before the liberation. The news of his death caused me great sadness.

Chapter Twenty-Eight

Feldafing

I moved to the camp there, recalling the past with people whose experiences were so similar to mine, I began to feel alive again. And there, though her brothers had not seen her since the selection in Auschwitz, I began to dream the impossible dream that Helen had also survived and that I would build my future with her.

With people speaking several different languages from all over Europe constantly arriving and departing, the displacement camp was like a railroad station. One day, passing a group speaking in Yiddish and Russian, I suddenly felt as if I had been hit over the head, the sound of Russian triggering memories of Schoemberg. Joining the group, I learned they were from a Russian repatriation camp of approximately one thousand in the nearby small town of Trouchgau. Before individuals from the camp were returned to Russia, a commission verified their identity, seeking to uncover those who collaborated voluntarily with the Germans. I felt strongly that Pitka might be in the camp. On the pretense that I was looking for friends, I asked if I could accompany the group back to Trouchgau the next morning. Traveling by American army truck, they said it would be the decision of the soldiers.

That night I could not sleep, thinking of my friend Lester and the countless others Pitka had killed, including so many of his own people. Lester's dying words rang in my ears, "Pitka is responsible for my death. If you survive, take revenge." I remembered my friend, the only one who gave me strength in the dark days of suffering to go on living with hope for a tomorrow.

Upon arriving at the repatriation camp, I saw before me thousands of Russians doing what so many of the Jews could not; dressed once again in the traditional clothing of their country, they prepared to go home. Jewish survivors waited for a country to open its doors and let us start a new life, a new beginning. Directed to the main office, to my great surprise, I found the person in charge of investigations before repatriation was Heniek Maliniak, a friend I studied with in Warsaw. Both of us were shocked at encountering each other in a Russian camp. I told him my reason for being there as several other people stood by and listened. We had been talking in Polish. A lot of people around us understood the language.

With Heniek accompanying me, I began to search for Pitka. It was not long before I spotted him. Among a group of people, he stood smiling, young and strong—a mass murderer. Staring at him in near disbelief, I raised my finger to indicate to Hemek which one he was. Reassuring me I need not worry, Heniek escorted me back to the office where he took out the files on Pitka. Then he turned to me and said, "It's late now. Tomorrow morning we'll take care of him."

Invited by Heniek to join him for dinner, I ate among Russian army officers, something I had not done before. After dinner, Heniek told me that in 1939 he fled Warsaw for Russia at which time, with his name not sounding Jewish, he passed as a non-Jew and began studies at the Russian university. Shortly thereafter he was sent first to a military academy, then the army. By the end of the war, he was given the rank of captain and put in charge of repatriation investigations.

In the morning, we found Pitka's body cut in two, his hands tied behind his back, laying in a pool of blood. Heniek speculated that the individuals who listened to me describe Pitka in his office took justice into their own hands.

Pitka's death gave me moral satisfaction. One of the mass murderers, at least, had paid for his crimes. So many did not. Living in Germany I saw those who had written the orders for slaughter now sit behind desks writing orders for the building of a new, financially stronger Germany. The anti-Semitic Germans were unchanged, and allowed us to remain in the country only due to external pressure, primarily from the American government. It was the United Nations Relief and Rehabilitation Agency (UNRRA) that supervised the displacement camps, providing food and clothing during the interim period after the war, and the Jewish community of the United States which assisted via the joint Distribution Committee UDC) and the ORT (Organization for Rehabilitation and Training), the latter creating trade schools for younger survivors.

Only a few days after the incident with Pitka, I experienced another shock. I learned from a group arriving from the death camp Mathausen that my brother Isaac had died a few days before the liberation. Returning to my room, I lay on my bed, closed my eyes, and silently prayed. "Lord, haven't I suffered enough? Have I lost everything? Please don't take away my last hope." A vision of Helen's face before me, I fell asleep.

During the next two weeks, tormented, sleepless, I waited and prayed for news of Helen. One day her brother Morris called out, "Joseph! Helen is alive!" It happened that a few people who had been to Radom let Morris know Helen was there with Henia Maliniak, their brother Sam's girlfriend.

When Morris told me he was returning to Poland to get Helen and Henia, I said I would go with him. In tears I thanked the Almighty for giving me back the gift of life.

The Polish committee in charge of returning citizens to Poland arranged papers for me within a few days. I bought a watch for Helen in Munich and headed for Radom with Morris on a Polish transport train.

Chapter Twenty-Nine

Return to Radom

I returned to the city in which I lost everything a human being has. Many of the street signs had been changed. Our houses remained, but the people were gone, the community destroyed, less than two hundred residing there now. As I walked by the house my parents once lived in, a chill went over me and I began to cry. I ran.

Since then I have not returned to Radom; the pain it caused me was too great. I was able to be there only in order to find Helen. It was painful to revisit the places of my past. Here I had spent my youth, had grown up, and now it was all nothing but memories. One family did survive, miraculously. The Den family. Having grown up with their son, Moniek, I stayed with them while in Radom, feeling I had a home again. I found out that one of my aunts, Nadia Gutman, my uncle Hiles's wife, had also survived.

Many Jews returned to Poland to find what remained after the Holocaust. The Polish, still hating us and having seen the Nazis kill millions, tried to finish off our community. In Radom the killing of Jews was a daily occurrence, and I witnessed several while there. Mr. Gudstat, inside his jewelry store, had his head chopped off by a Polish man who then flung the severed head onto the street. That same day the city's only Jewish tailor, who lived in his shop across from the police station on Zeromskiego Street, was also killed. For Jews, Poland was another slaughterhouse, like Germany, and most of us there waited for a chance to emigrate and live on soil not soaked with the blood of our people, and to begin a new life.

One day, returning to my parents' home, somewhat fearfully I asked the occupants for the furniture my father left to be safeguarded by them until the war ended. As I stood in the doorway talking with them, a Polish man came from within, shouting. In his hand was an ax. He threatened that if I did not leave, he would chop off my head. Terrified, I ran.

Chapter Thirty

Helen

It was summer. As I walked down Zeromskiego Street, I suddenly saw Helen a few feet ahead of me. In disbelief, I shook my head. Closing my eyes and reopening them I saw Helen standing, looking at me. My dream girl, her eyes dark and her face, which sustained me through my worst moments, so beautiful. My heart beat quickly. I could not get one word out. I could not believe it. I was frozen to the ground. I started to sweat; just looking at her, I was speechless.

At last I ran toward her, calling out her name, and with tears in my eyes, I embraced and kissed her. Gently pushing me away, she said my name. I was glad to know at least she remembered it. I felt so happy, having waited so long for this moment. My only goal now was to take care of her. I was happy again. Finally, we were reunited after so much pain and suffering which both of us had been through. We walked, talked, and shared moments from the past. She spoke, with tears in her eyes of how Fishel had not survived. I told her Isaac had not survived either.

With another survivor, Rubin Pasternak, I went to the cellar where my father had hidden money and jewelry. All told, we dug out some silver, gold, and British pounds.

After selling much of the stash to Moniek Rosenberg, a friend who owned a hardware store, I gave Rubin 100 American dollars. Once I finished putting together a belt with a pocket for my money, I went out and bought some nice clothes. Afterwards I asked Helen to go with me to buy her shoes, as the ones she wore, like her clothes, were quite worn. But she refused, saying if she needed something, her brothers would buy it. She had not accepted the watch either. Though I knew I was one of the few able to get money immediately after coming out of the death camps, I did not pressure Helen to accept my gifts.

Listening to our conversation, Henia said to me, "Joseph, give her time to get to know you again. We've been free only a few months and Helen is trying to find her own way to go on living. Remember, her search for her brother Fishel ended in finding he was gone." Deciding I would have to accustom myself to being patient, I proceeded with the business at hand of taking possession of property by my parents. But soon Helen told me she was leaving with Morris and Henia to join her other surviving brothers in the Feldafing displacement camp. Explaining that my parents' houses were in escrow at the moment, I tried to persuade her to stay with me a few more weeks until I had enough money to provide for us in the interim period of awaiting emigration. She was not persuaded. Her final word was that if I wanted to see her after completing my business in Radom, she would be with her brothers.

I had to make a quick decision. Henia warned me that if I stayed, I would end up with money, but would also lose Helen. Deeply upset, still I felt it was necessary to have money for our future. I would join them in a few weeks, I said.

Within a few days I sold the house on Zeromskiego Street. Paid partially in heavy gold pieces, I asked Mr. Den to safeguard the gold until the next summer when I planned to return. Then, extremely distraught over being separated from Helen and growing physically ill, I was persuaded by Mr. Den to give Mrs. Rottenberg power of attorney for the sale of the two remaining houses owned by my family. Thinking I had successfully taken care of business, I returned to Feldafing with a couple of friends, Lola Freidenreich and Majer Zajdenwber, who continued on from there to Stuttgart.

Reunited with Helen, I did not leave her for one moment. I was happy. Finally my dream came true. We had been walking for days, talking, building our future together. The more time I spent with her, the more my love for her grew. I understood that she was the partner with whom I would spend the rest of my life.

Helen and I became engaged after several weeks together in Feldafing and, on November 25, 1945 in the office of the Feldafing *Burgermeister*, were married according to civil law. On March 19, 1946 in a ceremony held in Munich's Deutsche Museum, we were married according to Jewish law.

My dream fulfilled, I returned to Radom to finish my business there. To my shock, I discovered I had been quite naive, to say the least. Mrs. Rottenberg, to whom I had given power of attorney, had sold my two houses, split the money with Mr. Den, and moved to Israel. From Mr. Den I could get no more than one-tenth of the gold I left with him for safekeeping. Though his son Moniek was a friend of mine, when I spoke with him about the matter he refused to intercede. Mrs. Den's response was the same. Furious, with no means of redress, I turned to my remaining resources. I sold another house and dug out more money from my father's stash in the cellar.

It was during this time that Polish hooligans killed forty-six survivors in Kielce. The situation in Poland had become untenable, and approximately two hundred and fifty thousand Jews soon left for Germany and Italy, en route to Israel.

Chapter Thirty-One

Munich

In 1946, at age 30, Helen, her brothers, and I moved from Feldafing to Munich. Persuaded by them to attend the university to finish my studies, in September of 1946 I stood before the entrance committee and was given an oral examination. I could not answer the professors' questions. Every word of my studies at the University of Warsaw had disappeared during the last several years of suffering. I ran from the room crying. It took me a year and a half to regain my memory.

It was in December of 1947 in the middle of the night that I awoke and suddenly was able to recall pages of poetry by Bialik, Heinrich Heine, Kochanowsky, Schiller. Ecstatic, I awakened Helen and told her. Yet, despite the return of my memory, I felt no desire to pursue studies at the university, particularly in medicine. The hospital in Schoemberg, where I saw so many people in horrible pain staring at me as I stood by helplessly, left me unable to bear the sight of wounds, of blood, of physical suffering. In later years, when our children became ill I could do nothing, only run from the room filled with horrible memories. I had told Helen before we were married that I would like to have a large family, with no idea at the time that so much of the responsibility for our children would be hers. Without her, I could not have realized my dreams.

In October of 1947, at the Munich city hall, I bought a street vendor's license to sell fruit and vegetables. With a three-wheeled cart, I stood on a corner of Mohlstrasse near the Jewish community center and sold watermelon and grapes. After a few months I began another business endeavor. Buying ten-year leases on several lots, I built stores which I then leased to others. The actual construction was a tricky business. I would go at night to the police station in the area where I wished to build a store, taking with me bottles of whiskey and cartons of American cigarettes. At the same time, my builders at the site poured a concrete foundation approximately 1,200 square feet, put up four posts, and nailed down a prefabricated roof. The next morning, going with a carpenter to the site, I finished the job, putting in walls, doors, and windows. Although I built these structures without a permit, I took advantage of a German law dating back many years, which stated that a foundation and roof, once in place, could not be moved.

The German authorities repeatedly tried legal measures to stop the construction. After finding German courts had no jurisdiction over me as a displaced person, they took me to an American court where, to their dismay, in each instance the judge approved continuation of construction. In a short time I was doing extremely well financially, having built twenty or so stores. I sold all of the stores except for two, which I kept. I ran one myself; the other store I ran with Mr. Schwartzberg. Exhausted from trying to be in two places at once, I soon sold my half to Mr. Schwartzberg.

With a warehouse full of coffee, cigarettes, nylons, and soap procured from the American PX, I sold goods which could not be obtained anywhere else at the time. From the Germans I procured butter and sugar for the store in exchange for these items. My stock was determined by law due to the food shortage in Bavaria at the time, so I could keep in the store one sack of coffee, one sack of sugar, and fifty pounds of butter. Wiedel, my German assistant, restocked items from the warehouse as I sold them. In 1949 at Easter I procured wine, the only store owner to do so at the time. The sidewalk and street outside my store was jammed with customers; in one week alone I sold 20,000 bottles of wine. To the traffic police I gave a bottle of wine and a pound of coffee each, a large gift as they were paid little for their work. I paid the police in this way on many occasions.

During these years Helen and I had two daughters, Lillian, born in 1946, and Rene, born in 1949. Helen, with the help of a nurse, took care of the children. At Helen's request, I sold one of the stores on Mohlstrasse to two of her brothers. The profit they made from it soon enabled them, with their wives, to emigrate to the United States.

Happy, with everything I could wish for in life, I thought little about the future but rather focused on the task at hand of earning money. A few weeks before Christmas, the traffic around the store quite heavy, I was engrossed in work until I turned and saw Helen standing with our daughter Lillian, then three and a half. Helen said she had something important to discuss. I asked her to wait, but she insisted. We went into my office and she said to Lillian, "Ask your father the same question you asked me coming home from school." With tears in her eyes our daughter asked, "Why don't I have cousins, uncles and aunts, and friends who visit me?" Helen turned to me and said, "Why did we come here? Germany is not the place for us to live and raise a family. We can't build our future here where our loved ones were murdered. Germany is a slaughterhouse. We have to go."

I asked, "Where? We have two beautiful children, a beautiful home, a good business, and plenty of money. What else would you like?"

"There's no future here for either us or our children," Helen said. "I would die if our daughters were to have German friends and marry Germans whose parents could be murderers of our loved ones. If you like it here, you can stay but I will try to take the children away from here. This place is full of terrible memories. Remember, my brother Fishel was murdered in Dachau. I can't raise our children in the shadows of death."

"Without you and the girls;" I said, "I wouldn't be able to live. You're all that matters to me. Wherever you go, I will go. Just give me time to go through the proper channels for us to emigrate to another country, and time to sell the business." The next morning I went to both the American and Australian consuls and applied to immigrate.

Thousands of Jews at this time were leaving Germany for the United States, South America, and Australia. While we waited to see which country would accept us, I reduced my inventory, by then housed in two warehouses. It was not an easy task. I sold the warehouses and store to a Yugoslavian man for a mere $350. In the meantime, having heard it was best to take to the United States silverware, fine china, and paintings, Helen and I purchased $7,000 worth of silver and porcelain and packed it in wooden crates.

More than one and a half years passed before the announcement came from the American consul that our application was approved. A week later, called in to pick up our visas, we found we had only forty-eight hours to get ready to travel to Bremen Haffen and from there to the United States. On the same day we left Bremen Haffen, an announcement of approval of our application for emigration came from the Australian consul.

Chapter Thirty-Two

Pasadena

On June 16, 1951 we landed at the port of New Orleans, Louisiana. From there we traveled by train to Pasadena, California, the City of Roses. I will never forget the people of Pasadena. Jews and non-Jews alike showed us such love and compassion. People from everywhere came to help us start a new life in the country where I am now so proud to be a citizen. My belief in humanity, which I had lost in the dark days of my life at the time of the Holocaust in Europe, I gained back here in this country. I believe, after all that I have been through there are still good people ready to help when help is needed. As a survivor, I was used to being pushed around by everyone. It was terribly degrading. Now, the people in America were trying to look after me, trying to help me. This was something new.

I had lived six long years in Germany after the liberation. Only with the help of the American administration could I go on living. After all, Germany is a cemetery for us survivors. I did not have another place to go. It was not so easy to live over there. Luckily, I came to the United States and I'm so glad. We have now found acceptance and love. All doors were opened to me. I took advantage and worked very hard. Slowly I started to open my eyes. I started to understand what it was like to live in America. My father made his fortune in real estate, and I followed in his footsteps. I went into real estate investment and development and, as well, opened a furniture store. Engrossed in providing for my family, the years seemed to go by quickly for me. Our son Louis was born in 1954, our daughter Cece in 1958.

Thanks to successful investments, we were able to pay for our children's education when they entered college. Lillian received a Master's in Social Work in 1968 and a year later, Rene received a Master's in Family Counseling. In 1978 Louis received his bachelor's and was accepted to study at a school of dentistry, while Cece finished her undergraduate studies. I was looking around and discovering that my children had all grown up.

The birds having left the nest, Helen and I were alone in a big house. Looking back I realized that, always busy with work, I had spent little time with our children, and had missed the opportunity to have close relationships with them. I discussed my feelings with Helen and then, hoping it was not too late, I began to spend time with our two daughters living in the area, Lillian and Rene. Talking with them, trying to under-stand them, I felt very proud of how bright these two women were. With sadness I realized Helen must have needed me at times when our children were growing up, yet I was not there. Without thinking, I simply lived according to the conventions I was brought up with, the ways I knew for survival. It took me many years to understand the nature of the society and era I had become part of and to adjust to the changing roles of men and women. Once I did, I liked it better. I felt happier being close to Helen, having her share with me the good times and the bad times.

In the United States I tried to forget my past. The rare times I had to face it were when our children were young and sometimes asked during the holidays why they had no grandparents. How can one explain to a child six or seven years of age that one's parents were murdered by Nazis? I simply said that bad people had killed our loved ones and, unable to speak of it further, I ran from the room, not wanting them to see my tears, my pain. Occasionally, I did tell them of my youth in the old country, of my grandfather's house, of my bar mitzvah, of our culture that no longer existed. I felt horrible pain over not telling them the truth about what had happened, yet I wanted to protect them and wanted them to have a normal childhood.

Chapter Thirty-Three

Broken Silence

In September 1978 when my wife and I attended a lecture by Elie Wiesel on the Holocaust, the past I had been trying to forget came back. With words he painted a picture of our suffering and, for a moment, tears came to my eyes and I had the uncanny feeling that it was me who was sharing the pain and suffering with the audience. For a moment I forgot where I was. I said to myself, "Joe, what in the world are you doing here? Your place is in front of the people, talking, sharing the past." I was sitting, swallowing every word. This man was showing me my destiny. Finally, after so many years I had found my road in life-the road of sharing what I had been through.

After the lecture, several people asked questions. The answer Elie Wiesel gave to "Why did the Jews go like sheep to their death?" did not satisfy me. I stood up. "Mr. Wiesel, though you and I both went through death camps there was a difference between us. You were fourteen at the time, whereas I was a young man, a university student, and this difference of age caused us to react differently to our circumstances. I would like your permission to give my own answer to the question."

Invited by Elie Wiesel I went up to the front and spoke before the audience. With a trembling voice, I began. "In the death camps, physically we were dead. Only the spiritual power in believing kept us going. We believed that somehow we would survive. You don't need a gun to fight, to help your fellow man, giving him courage to go on living. Telling him to go on, not to give in, to share your piece of bread with a hungry friend, to give him a hand when he was laying on the ground—this was resistance. Believing in a tomorrow in the place of pain was a *Waffen* which kept us going. It is impossible to believe that this was our *Waffen*—the belief in God when God was dead. Only the belief was there in this place of living hell." I continued for a few more minutes.

It was my first time speaking publicly of the Holocaust, my first time answering the disturbing question of why our people passively went to death. As I returned to my seat, I silently remembered the millions who died in the death camps.

Soon afterward, receiving invitations from various organizations to lecture on the Holocaust, I began to speak publicly of my personal experiences as well as the general circumstances of the Jewish people. Finding I could not answer some of the questions concerning historical and political issues surrounding the Holocaust, I educated myself in this area, reading books and attending lectures of scholars in the field. Dormant for so many years, my hunger for knowledge returned.

After closing my business, I would study at home late into the night. I saw that there were more important things in life than money. I lost a bit of my touch in business but I saw that for years I had forgotten where I truly belong: my wealth was now the wealth of knowledge. I had started down this road as a university student, the road which I had missed but where I belonged. Finally, I had found my purpose in life.

One night at twelve o'clock I received a call from my son, Louis, who was a student at Northwestern University. The hour being late, I knew something was wrong. Louis told me that a professor at the university had lectured that afternoon, claiming that the Holocaust never happened. The lecturer, a certain Professor Butz, said Jews had invented the story of the Holocaust, that it was a hoax. It was very disturbing for my son to listen to, that an educated man who had access to sources of finding the truth was trying to revise the pages of history. "I remember," Louis said, "Just before my bar mitzvah you told me about our people being tortured and burned to death in ovens at Auschwitz." I said, "Your mother and I were in Auschwitz. We smelled the burning flesh. Your mother saw her friends taken to the crematorium, she saw the ovens inside, she saw the boxes of ashes dragged out and thrown into the river. What Professor Butz said is not true."

Helen told Louis as well that the professor's lecture was a lie. After the conversation ended, Helen and I could not sleep, but rather spent the rest of the night discussing how it was possible for a university professor to teach such lies, to revise history. It was our first encounter with a denial of the Holocaust and it reinforced my commitment to speak publicly of my experiences.

Struggling with my heavy schedule, I continued to run my business, to study, and to give lectures on Sundays and sometimes on weekdays when I closed the store early. Time seemed to pass very quickly. Then in 1980 at Passover, the table set for the seder, I sat talking with my wife and three daughters as we awaited the arrival of my son and future daughter-in-law. The phone rang. I answered and heard a man's voice say, "You stinking Jew. Stop talking if you want to live. Otherwise we'll kill you." Thinking it was a prank, I hung up. After a few minutes, again the phone rang. The same voice, "Remember, you dirty Jew. Get the message? Shape up or we'll kill you."

Frightened and shaking, I told my family. The phone rang

again and one of my daughters answered. Finding it was the same man, she asked who he was, why he was calling. He repeated the threat. Calling the sheriff's office, we were informed that without the phone number of the caller nothing could be done.

The next morning at the police station two blocks from my furniture business, I requested protection. For the next two months the police checked on my store every few hours, stopping their car in front. At times a plainclothesman dropped by the store for a few minutes.

I continued to lecture and, after a while, forgot about the calls. After a few months, coincidental with a newspaper notice about my upcoming lecture to B'nai B'rith Youth, an employee at my store received a call in which the threats were repeated. Undaunted, I gave the lecture. That was the last threat the caller made.

It had taken me many years to be able to speak of the Holocaust and to relive it. My system had needed time to forget. Elie Wiesel, through his lectures and his writings, helped me come to understand my role in society as a Holocaust survivor, as witness to the crimes against the Jewish people, as one whose voice could warn of what can come of hatred and bigotry.

In 1981 I liquidated my furniture business. As a result I had more time to study. With Helen's encouragement and a hundred books on the Holocaust in my library, I spent many hours preparing for my lectures. As she attended my lectures, Helen's comments helped me improve my manner of relating to the audience. After a while, she joined me in lecturing, and the two of us shared the story of our romance. It is the story of two young people, their suffering as they had been separated in the Auschwitz death camp, the long nights in the extermination camps full of pain and inhuman suffering, and the unbroken will in believing which kept us going in the places of the living dead. At the end, by a miracle, we survived and met again and started a new life full of hope for a better tomorrow.

Often I cried during my lectures, though less frequently as time went by and I learned to gain control over my emotions. We survivors do have feelings, though the Nazis tried to kill all emotion in us. It is miraculous that after what we went through, we still act normally, still dream, still realize our dreams.

Attending a survivors' convention in Washington, D.C. in 1983, I heard for the first time of the Martyrs' Memorial and Museum of the Holocaust in Los Angeles. Regina Hertel, a docent at the museum, told me of her work and asked if I would be interested in participating. I agreed to visit after the end of the convention. Once at the museum, I immediately felt my work was there. In addition to my lectures, I had the opportunity of meeting scholars from all over the world and continuing my studies utilizing the library housed next to the museum. At this time Shalmi Barmori, the Director of Education at Yad Vashem in Jerusalem, had taken a sabbatical leave to direct the Museum of the Holocaust in Los Angeles. Possessing a wealth of knowledge on the Holocaust, the views of this Israeli-born scholar had a clarity that was difficult for me to attain as one who had suffered so much personally. Through attending his lectures and reading books he recommended, my interpretation of the Holocaust changed. Until I met him I was living in the Holocaust trauma. This man woke me and took me from my past. As an Israeli and an individual of a free society, he enabled me to understand the tragedy which had touched me so deeply.

I began to view and speak of the Holocaust from a broader

perspective, as a tragedy of Western civilization. I began to speak of the horrors of the Holocaust not out of anger or desire for revenge, but out of desire for something to be learned, for humanity to better its future. That year I lectured to more than five hundred students in schools in the Los Angeles area and to Jewish children in Camp Rammath. I was able to share with them my terrible past. I saw in front of me our children, our future. This was what Hitler and his henchmen tried to destroy. Here I was, the past reaching out to them, building in front of them a better future not only for Jewish people but for the whole Western world.

In the next several years of studying, lecturing, and working as a docent at the museum, I at last came to feel I had found the correct way to express myself and to interpret the Holocaust.

Chapter Thirty-Four

Return to the Ruins

Helen and I felt a moral obligation to show the place of our beginnings to at least one of our children. We tried to raise them as normal children. But they did not have the pleasure of playing with their cousins, they never knew the gentle touch of their grandfather's hand, or the sweet smile and the voice of their grandmother. The Nazis robbed them of this pleasure. Now that they were grown up, it was time to share with them our terrible yesterdays. In the summer of 1984, Helen, Cece, and I accompanied a group of Los Angeles community leaders, among them Rabbi Chaim Seidler Felle, on a visit to the ruins of once-thriving Eastern European Jewish communities.

Our visit to Auschwitz was very difficult for Helen. Memories of the painful experiences and the smell of burning flesh returned. My wife, my daughter Cece, and I stood together at the edge of the artificial lake made by the Nazis, the lake into which they threw sixty thousand boxes of our loved ones' ashes when they no longer had time to send them to Germany to be made into fertilizer for growing vegetables. Standing there I caught sight of a bone of a small child. I picked it up. As I held it in my hand, I thought of how it could be a bone of one of my cousins burned in the Auschwitz crematorium. I cried. As I looked up I saw my daughter watching with tears in her eyes. This was a communication without words. My daughter was reliving the pain and suffering with me. This moment was very painful for me. After so many years I was still suffering.

Warsaw was the city in which I received my university education, a city with a Jewish community of a few hundred where there had once been over half a million. Once there, Helen, Cece, and I visited the monument to the heroes of the ghetto uprising led by Mordechai Amelewicz. Their armed resistance, though they knew it was futile, was a symbol of the revival of the Jewish people, the revival which not long afterwards brought about the state of Israel, the end of the *Staadose Jude* (the stateless Jew). Though six million died, at last there is a country in which we can live under self-rule, a right denied during the Holocaust and for centuries prior to that terrible time.

In Radom, as Helen and I brought Cece to the houses we grew up in, I felt a chill run through me. The houses remained, but our loved ones were gone. Looking at the structures was like looking at a graveyard. Where once a synagogue had been situated across from Helen's house, there was now only an empty lot. Approaching Helen's house, we passed a group of young Polish people. One of the men yelled, "I didn't know there were any Jews still alive! If Hitler didn't kill them all, we'll finish the job!" As I raised my hand to strike this loudmouth, Dr. Shapiro, a friend accompanying us, stopped me. "Joe, let it go. Look where we are. This is Poland, not America. They can kill us. Calm down. Forget about it."

I was enraged at the thought of the new generation of Poles who learned nothing from the past nor of the crimes of their parents' generation. During the war only four thousand or so out of a Polish population of thirty million are known to have aided the Jews. Most turned Jews over to the Nazis for a mere pound of butter or salami. Eighty percent of the Jewish population of Poland was killed.

Of the countries we visited in Eastern Europe, Hungary alone still had a thriving Jewish community. One hundred thousand Jews lived in Budapest. At the city's Jewish Theological Institute, I spoke with the dean, Professor Scheiber, one of the few surviving religious scholars from the yeshiva in Vilna. I had recently learned to videotape in order to supplement my lectures, and was therefore able to record his perspective on the Holocaust. Two years later he passed away. While there I also had the opportunity to speak with a few of the institute's rabbinical students from Russia. I was struck by the fact that a communist regime allowed Jews to leave the country to undertake religious studies and return as community religious leaders.

Arriving back in California, with assistance from the Museum of the Holocaust, I had the videotape of our trip professionally edited. Continuing to tape interviews as well as lectures that Helen and I gave, I eventually acquired a studio and did my own editing of over twenty-five, videos on the Holocaust. These videos, primarily housed in the museum, will serve as testimony to future generations of one nation's crime in this century, a crime which was committed against its own citizens whose only fault was that they had been born of a particular religion. The tapes will also serve as an educational tool to teach the worst consequences of bigotry, intolerance, and hatred.

Chapter Thirty-Five

Gates of Tomorrow

Following our trip, Helen spoke more freely of the past to me and to the public. The thousands of letters we received in the next few years gave us both courage to continue lecturing on the horrors we had been through. It was never easy. As lecturers for both the Museum of the Holocaust and the Anti-Defamation League of B'nai B'rith (ADL) we talked to students of all ages. Unfortunately, the audience at times was quite hostile.

In 1985 when Shalmi Barmori returned to his position at Yad Vashem, Michael Nutkiewicz, a history professor and a child of survivors, became director of the Museum of the Holocaust. I learned a lot from our director by attending his lecture series on the history of the Holocaust. It was unusual that a scholar, historian, and a child of a survivor had a way to interpret the Holocaust in such a way that the public or the reader can understand the tragedy and the importance of what happened at the time of the *Shoah* (Hebrew word for Holocaust).

In May 1987 I went with Helen to Israel, traveling to several historical sites to witness the history of our people along with Shalmi Barmori. Now I understood better the history of my people as explained by Shalmi, who as a *sabra* (native Israeli) was far removed from any first-hand experience with the Holocaust. In October of 1987, I spoke before an audience of two hundred or so students and several faculty members at Redlands High School in California. As I described the moment on April 26, 1945 when the American soldier brought me to consciousness, from the back of the auditorium a voice called out, "I'm the soldier who was with you!" Bernard Lowry of Redlands, California, was indeed among the American troops who found me and helped bring me back to life. This man, who now taught at the high school, joined me at the podium. We embraced and cried, both of us overcome with emotion. What a moment. Forty-two years afterwards, thousands of miles away, I found the man who liberated me, the man who lifted me from the ground when I lay dying. After a few moments, I asked if he would like to speak of his experience to the audience. In a trembling voice, he said, "Though it was a long time ago, it is still painful for me to recall. After the bombing of Pearl Harbor, at age eighteen I enlisted in the army and was sent to Germany. Though I had been brought up not to kill another human being, I suddenly had a gun in my hand and was fighting a war, a war to liberate the prisoners and the world at large from fanatics who had caused society so much damage. When I saw for myself so many innocent people inflicted with such misery, it became clear to me why we had been sent to liberate the prisoners, to liberate people like this man." Turning to me with tears in his eyes, he embraced me and, for a moment, was unable to speak.

"Photographs my friends took as we liberated the camps," he continued, "I kept in a drawer for many years, unable to look at them. After a while, I threw them into the fire. The memories were too painful. Now, looking at Joe, I remember again the pain I felt as human skeletons lay all around us. Most of the people in the camps were not as fortunate as Joe. So many died." He started to cry again and said he was unable to talk anymore.

I spoke to the audience. "This man and I have memories of a happy moment we shared which will remain with us forever. His was the hand to give me my first drink of water as I lay dying. An American soldier, he gave me back my life and was, my symbol of freedom. Today my wife and I, two Holocaust survivors, and an American soldier stand before you, witnesses to a part of Western history. Remember what happened to us, learn from the past, never forget what hatred and bigotry can do."

A year later, with a professional video crew, I made a tape of myself and the man who liberated me, a tape which has since been used internationally for educational purposes. Now I not only lecture, but travel, taping interviews of world leaders. We are fortunate enough to have the tools to preserve the truth about events which should never be forgotten. The Holocaust, I have found, is being denied with increasing frequency.

In 1989 the Museum of the Holocaust held an ADL sponsored symposium for the children of survivors and of perpetrators. The two groups exchanged views, trying to comprehend the tragedy of their inheritance. Listening to both sides, I felt it an honor to be present at this event in which young people reached out to each other to build bridges of understanding. I recorded the session on video.

Not long afterwards, Helen and I interviewed one of the panel members, the daughter of a general of the *Waffen* SS. I began the interview as follows: "Remember that you have in front of you two Holocaust survivors and that you are the daughter of a man who was a perpetrator, a man who gave orders to kill my loved ones. It took a great deal of courage for us to interview you. We do so because you are among the young generation of Germans trying to find answers about the past, to deal with what happened, to prevent repeating the mistakes, to build a better tomorrow based on love and understanding of all regardless of race or religion. Listening to you at the symposium gave me the feeling I was listening to the voice of reason in Germany that was lacking in the past. I hope there will be more voices like yours, with new ideas for a tomorrow in which all people are free."

As this woman expressed to us the views of many of her generation, I gained moral satisfaction despite how painful it was to recall the events with her. Helen and I overcame our difficulties, feeling it was our duty to listen to the voice of Germany today.

I still have much work before me, including completion of a video on Anne Frank, who was the inspiration for this book. In making the video I traveled to Kyoto, Japan, to visit a house dedicated to her, and to Amsterdam, Holland, to visit the house she once lived in, now a museum in her name. There I interviewed visitors to the museum who came from all over the world. For Helen and me, her house seemed a shrine, and to be there was quite an emotional experience.

Many years have passed since I started to lecture. I feel that I have learned a lot, but still I am studying and reading many books. So much information about the Holocaust has become available since the dissolution of the Soviet Union. I still have a desire to study. This is a long road which I chose. I have no regrets. At this moment I still work at the Museum of the Holocaust in Los Angeles. I have so much to learn, and now I have not so much time in which to learn.

I have come to the end of my book. In it I have shared with you my life story full of tears and at times joy. There were moments when I gave up. I am glad I found the strength to continue and to finish it. Despite the years of studying and lecturing, the question "Why?" remains with me.

Glossary

A

APPEL the counting of inmates in the concentration camp.
ARBEITSAMT employment office.
ARBEITSCHEINE labor card.
ABBEITSLAGGER labor camp.

B

BAHNHOF railroad station.
BAR MITZVAH a ceremony recognizing a Jewish boy of the age thirteen as attaining adult status.
BLOCKELDER block supervisor.
B'NAI B'RITH a Jewish social and political organization.
BUG RIVER a river running north-south in Poland, which divided Nazi and Soviet Forces after the Non-Aggression Pact of 1939.
BURGERMEISTER mayor of a city.

C

CELNIKER DOCTOR was working at the dental office with my brother in Radom on Szkolna.
CHALLAH special braided bread for Sabbath meals.
CHEDER a Hebrew school.
CYNA BROTHERS the only ones who escaped on the death march in 1944.

D

DACHAU death camp in Bayen Germany.
DIASPORA term for Jews living outside the State of Israel.

E, F

FRANK, ANNE was a young teenager from Holland who spent most of the war years hidden from the Nazis in an attic. She perished in a death camp toward the end of the war. Her diary remains a moving piece of literature on the Holocaust.

G

GHETTO CLINIC a room only at the hospital in the small ghetto in Radom, which have been used for emergency service.

GLINICE name of a suburb in Radom.

GLINICE GHETTO the small ghetto was establish in March 1941 in the suburb of Glinice. (Radom)

H

HAFTORAH a part from the book of Prophets which has been read every Saturday morning in the shul after reading the Torah at the Jewish services.

HOLOCAUST (also known as the Catastrophe, the SHO'AH, Hurban in Hebrew) is the most tragic period of Jewish Diaspora history and modern mankind as a whole.

K

KADDISH Jewish prayers recited by mourners for deceased love ones.

KAPO Jewish police in the concentration camps.

KIDDUSH HA-SHEM (lit., "sanctifying the Name of God") Hebrew term that was used in postbiblical Jewish history to denote exemplary ethical conduct and that became applied to religious martyrdom.

KISHENOV a city in the Ukraine, Russia.

KOSZARY in Polish Station place for the Polish army.

KOVNO a city in Poland before 1939.

KRANKENHAUS German word for hospital.

KROMOLOWSKY PLACE where I was working after the liquidation the ghetto in Radom 1942.

L

LAGERELDER superviser over the kapos in the death camp.

LAGERFUHRER German official in charge of death camps.

M

MAJDANEK death camp in Poland.

MATHAUSEN death camp in Germany.

MENGELE German doctor in charge of the selection of Auschwitz, also known as the "ANGEL OF DEATH."

MOHLSTRASSE a street in Munich Germany.

N

NUREMBERG LAWS two constitutional laws issued on September 15, 1935, that became the basis for the legal exclusion of Jews from German life and the ensuring anti Jewish policy.

O

OBSADA department at the amunition factory where my brother worked.

P

PENTZ GARDEN a place in Radom, where the SS buried our love-ones murdered at the liquidation of the city Radom in 1942.

PERETZA STREET a name of a street in Radom.

POGROM attack on Jews by the local population.

R

RADOM the city where I was born.

RYNEK name of a street in Radom.

S

SCHOEMBERG death camp in Germany.

SEDER a family feast to celebrate the exodus of the Jews from Egypt during Biblical times.

SHEMA YISRAEL Hebrew words, the beginning of a Jewish prayer.

SHOAH a Hebrew word for the Holocaust.

SHUL a Jewish house of worship.

SIDDUR a Jewish prayer book.

SONDERKOMMANDOS a military unit of the SS whose task was to obliterate evidence of mass slaughter by opening burial pits and burning the corpses they contained.

STAATLOSE JUDE a Jew without a country.

STASZOW a little town in Poland.

STATE MIASTO a street in Radom.

ST. KAZIMIERZA name of a hospital in Radom.

STURBAHNFUHRER rank of a major in the German army.

SZPITALNA Street a street in Radom.

SZWARLIKOWSKA a street in Radom.

SZYDLOWIECZ a small town in Poland.

T

TIKKUN CHACOT midnight prayer commemorating the destruction of the Jewish temple in Jerusalem by the Romans.

TISHAH B'AB a Jewish holiday commemorating the destruction of the temple in Jerusalem.

TOMASZOW a name of a city in Poland.

Torah the Jewish Bible.

Tzedaka a Hebrew word for charity

V

VOLKSDEUTSCH a German living outside Germany.

W

WAFFEN a German word for arms.

WALOWA STREET name of a street in Radom.

WARSAW Capital of Poland.

WASZAWSKA STREET name of a street in Radom.

WEHRMACHT a German word for army.

WIESEL, ELIE a teacher, philosopher, world-known writer, Nobel Peace prize laureate and also the Chairman of the Holocaust Survivors.

WITKOWSKY DOCTOR at the hospital in Radom. He was in charge of the hospital in 1939 where I was working.

Y

YAD VASHEM Holocaust Museum in Jerusalem.

YESHIVA a Jewish school for boys studying the Talmud.

Z

ZAMLYNIA STREET a name of a street in Radom.

ZEROMSKIEGO STREET a name of a street in Radom.

ZYNTIA a name of a street in Radom.

Sources: Encyclopedia of the Holocaust (New York: Macmillan Publishing Co.); Encyclopaedia judaica Uerusalem, Israel).